The State of Modern-Day Human Rights

From the Women, Peace and Security Act to Atrocity Prevention

William J. Manosh

2025

Copyright © 2025 William J. Manosh

All rights reserved.

No part of this book may be reproduced, stored in a retrieval system, or transmitted in any form or by any means—electronic, mechanical, photocopying, recording, or otherwise—without prior written permission of the author, except for brief quotations used in reviews or scholarly discussion.

First edition: 2025

Printed and bound in the United States of America

Manosh Press

ISBN: 979-8-9944510-2-1 (paperback)

For my sweet wife and life partner of 16 years.

Table Of Contents

Chapter 1: Mapping Trump-Era Human Rights 4

Chapter 2: Women, Peace, and Security and Atrocity Prevention Frameworks 15

Chapter 3: Post–Cold War Globalism, Relativism, and the Human-Rights System 31

Chapter 4: Venezuela: Repression, Sanctions, and the Limits of Protection 42

Chapter 5: Xinjiang: Surveillance, Genocide Claims, and Algorithmic Authoritarianism.. 55

Chapter 6: Islamic Human Rights, Cultural Relativism, and the Middle East 68

Chapter 7: Borders as a Human-Rights Test 81

Chapter 8: Human Rights in a Transactional World: What has changed in 2025, and Why................................102

References... 111

About the Author 130

Chapter 1: Mapping Trump-Era Human Rights

When people in Washington talk about "human rights," they rarely mean just one thing. The terminology can point to atrocities prevention, sanctions on Chinese officials over Xinjiang, protections for trafficking survivors, or just as often laws that restrict the rights of migrants in the name of security. Under both Trump administrations, that discourse is not a side story; but is the story. This book treats the Trump years as an example for the modern human-rights discourse built upon since the late 20th century. Rather than starting with victims and working outward, this first chapter starts with how human-rights policy is actually developed in the United States, and how the CIA, State Department, Congress, and the White House work together. The goal here is simple: to give you a clear explanation of the legal and institutional mechanisms so that later chapters in Venezuela, Xinjiang, and migration detention, have credibility.

There is no single statute in the U.S. Code labeled "The Human Rights Act." Instead, human rights appear in a menagerie of laws that imply foreign and domestic policies in different manners. For purposes of this book, Trump-era "human-rights laws" fall into three main categories:

Foreign-policy human-rights

These are the most visible in Trump's first term:

- Women, Peace, and Security Act of 2017 (Pub. L. 115-68) – commits the U.S. to promoting women's participation in peace and security processes[1].
- Elie Wiesel Genocide and Atrocities Prevention Act (Pub. L. 115-441) – declares atrocity prevention a U.S. national

interest and mandates training, early-warning, and coordinated strategies[2].

These laws translate basic human-rights language into sanctions, reporting requirements, and diplomatic positions focused upon other governments.

Cross-cutting rights and "modern day slavery" laws

These have had wide bipartisan support and remain across administrations:

- The Frederick Douglass Trafficking Victims Prevention and Protection Reauthorization Act of 2018 renewed and expanded U.S. anti-trafficking programs at home and abroad[8].
- Ongoing reauthorizations in Trump's second term, such as H.R. 1144 in 2025, show how trafficking is framed as a moral consensus issue rather than a partisan battleground[9].
- Domestic civil-rights–implicating laws in Trump II In the second Trump administration, the biggest statutory moves so far are not classic human-rights expansions, but are emphasized as:
- The Laken Riley Act (Pub. L. 119-1), mandating detention of certain non-citizens and enabling state lawsuits against the federal government over enforcement failures[10].
- The Epstein Files Transparency Act[12], compelling disclosure of DOJ records on Jeffrey Epstein and Ghislaine Maxwell subject to privacy and security limits[11].

These laws operate within U.S. territory, thus shaping migrants' due-process rights on one hand and victims' access to information on the other[13]. Throughout this book, when I refer to "human-rights law" in the Trump era, I'm talking about this combined human rights system foreign-facing accountability, atrocity prevention discourse, trafficking and exploitation protections, and domestic laws that either expand or contract the rights of people within U.S. jurisdiction.

The Institutional Machinery: Who Actually Does What?

Congress: Where Human-Rights Language Becomes Law

Congress is the only actor that can create binding statutes like the Uyghur Act or the Laken Riley Act. But the process is fragmented:

Committees

- Foreign Relations / Foreign Affairs committees generally lead on foreign human-rights bills.
- Judiciary and Homeland Security committee shape immigration and civil rights legislation.
- Appropriations committees attach human-rights conditions or reporting requirements to funding bills, including defense and foreign operations.

Bipartisan coalitions

Several Trump-era human-rights laws came from cross-party sponsorship:

Rubio (R-FL) led both the Hong Kong and Uyghur laws, but with heavy Democratic co-sponsorship[15] (2019).

Rep. Chris Smith (R-NJ) led the Frederick Douglass trafficking law, a classic example of "moral consensus" legislation (Frederick Douglass Trafficking Victims Prevention and Protection Reauthorization Act of 2018, 2018).

Oversight tools

Beyond statutes, Congress uses:

- Reporting requirements in laws like the Elie Wiesel Act and Uyghur Act, forcing the executive branch to periodically document abuses and U.S. responses [17].
- Hearings and subpoenas to interrogate State, CIA, and Defense officials about human-rights crises—sometimes as genuine oversight, sometimes as political discourse. In this book, "legislative traction" means more than just bills introduced. It means laws actually passed and signed, with enough useful measures: sanctions, reports, funding conditions that can shape U.S. behaviors and policies.

The State Department: Human-Rights Narrator-in-Chief

If Congress drafts the manuscript, the State Department performs them publicly.

Country Reports on Human Rights Practices:

- Each year, State's Bureau of Democracy, Human Rights, and Labor produce a separate report for nearly every country, describing "significant human rights issues" ranging from extrajudicial killings and torture to restrictions on civil society[19]. These reports are mandated by Congress and are a primary reference for:
- Sanctions decisions under the Global Magnitsky Act and country-specific laws.
- Certification requirements in legislation like the Hong Kong Act and Uyghur Act.
- Congressional debates, NGO advocacy, and litigation strategies.
- Atrocity prevention and early warning.

The Elie Wiesel Act requires the executive branch to maintain and improve early- warning mechanisms for mass atrocities and to train diplomats accordingly (Elie Wiesel

Genocide and Atrocities Prevention Act of 2018, 2018). In practice:

- State coordinates with the intelligence community to assess risk in places like
- Those assessments feed into sanctions (like the Caesar Act) and diplomatic moves.

Diplomatic messaging

Secretaries of State use human-rights language in speeches, press statements, and bilateral meetings. During Trump's first term, for example, Xinjiang was cast as a "stain of the century" even as other abusive partners, such as Saudi Arabia or Egypt, often faced softer public criticism[20]. For this books purposes, State is the public narrator of U.S. human-rights policy: it names abuses, ranks their severity and often proposes legislation for a global audience.

The Intelligence Community and the CIA: Quiet Backbone

The Central Intelligence Agency and the wider U.S. intelligence community rarely appear by name in statutes, but they are irreplaceable to how human-rights laws are implemented.

Factual input for reports and sanctions

Country reports, atrocity-prevention risk assessments, and sanctions designations all depend on classified and open-source intelligence: satellite imagery of mass detention facilities, intercepted communications, internal regime documents, and more. Target selection and impact analysis, sanctions laws often require the President or the Secretary of State to designate specific individuals or entities. The intelligence community helps identify who actually matters, which Chinese tech companies, which Venezuelan security units. In the Xinjiang context, for example, intelligence reporting helped corroborate NGO and media evidence about the scale of detention and surveillance, which then informed both the Uyghur Act and Magnitsky sanctions Intelligence also evaluates and measures effects of sanctions and whether they are deterring abusive actors or are they shifting these to civilian populations.

Covert and gray-zone activity

This book is not meant to speculate about classified operations, but it is important to note that statutes like the Caesar Act or Venezuela sanctions exist alongside covert tools that are not available in public laws. These legal and covert measures are therefore not just one part of the extensive CIA and State Defense mechanisms for responding to or exploiting human-rights crises. Summarily, while State provides the language and Congress provides the law, the CIA often provides the evidence and the targets.

The White House and the President: Agenda-Setter and Gatekeeper

No human-rights law becomes law without the chief executive's signature unless Congress can provide the votes to override a veto, which is rare and uncommon. Under Trump, the presidency plays several critical roles:

Signing or blocking statutes

In the first term, Trump signed a suite of bipartisan human-rights laws—often with little public fanfare. The WPS Act, Elie Wiesel Act, Caesar Act, Hong Kong

Act, Uyghur Act, and Tibet provisions were all enacted on his watch (Women,

Peace, and Security Act of 2017, 2017; Hong Kong Human Rights and

Democracy Act of 2019, 2019; Uyghur Human Rights Policy Act of 2020, 2020).

in the second term, he signed the Laken Riley Act enthusiastically, presenting it as a law-and-order victory, and signed the Epstein Files Transparency Act under intense bipartisan and public pressure (Laken Riley Act, 2025; Epstein Files Transparency Act, 2025; Khanna, 2025).

Executive orders and regulatory changes

Many of the most consequential human rights decisions never pass through Congress. They become law through:

- Executive orders on refugees, visas, and migration enforcement.
- Regulatory changes to asylum procedures or civil-rights enforcement metrics.
- Budget proposals and internal guidance that alter how aggressively existing human-rights and civil-rights laws are implemented.

Symbolic and rhetorical choices

The President frequently decides when human rights are front-and-center and when they are not:

North Korea: human-rights atrocities dominated early rhetoric, then faded during summit diplomacy.

Saudi Arabia: despite the murder of Jamal Khashoggi, arms sales and strategic priorities largely prevailed.

China: human-rights condemnation intensified as strategic and economic tensions escalated.

This book describes the presidency as both a gatekeeper (of which laws become reality) and signal generator (who "deserves" U.S. human-rights attention and who does not).

Trump as Stress Test: Continuity and Break

The Trump years are built upon layers of previous leadership. They sit on top of decades of human-rights discourse built under both Republican and Democratic administrations. To better make sense of what is distinctive about Trump I and Trump II, it helps to separate continuities from breaks.

Continuities

Annual human-rights reporting continued without interruptions. The Country Reports on Human Rights Practices remained a central tool for documenting abuses worldwide[23]. Trafficking policy remained a bipartisan priority. The Frederick Douglass Act and its reauthorizations fit squarely in the trajectory launched by the original Trafficking Victims Protection Act in 2000[21]. Atrocity prevention gained formal statutory basis with the Elie Wiesel Act, building upon earlier executive initiatives rather than rejecting them (Elie Wiesel Genocide and Atrocities Prevention Act of 2018, 2018). Within these specific human rights concerns, Trump's first term looks more like identification and reprioritization than a complete dismantling.

Breaks

Selective enforcement and "America First" filtering

Migration and asylum policies shift sharply toward deterrence and exclusion, culminating in term-two legislation like the

Laken Riley Act that embeds mandatory detention into statute. Feminist security initiatives created by the WPS Act have already come under attack as "woke" by Trump-aligned officials, despite having been signed into law during his own first term[24].

Geopolitical targets

China, Iran, Venezuela, and North Korea became focal points of human-rights rhetoric and legislation because they had aligned with pre-existing strategic contests, not because they were uniquely abusive in the global landscape. By contrast, key security partners with serious abuses—Saudi Arabia, Egypt, the Philippines, did not face any significant legislative interest. The Trump era seems less about abolishing human-rights tools and more about weaponizing them selectively, amplification of some human rights crises and overlooking some others. To make sense of this menagerie of laws, institutions, and politics, the chapters that follow will utilize a few recurring concepts.

Legislative traction

A human-rights cause has "traction" when it:

- Is repeatedly highlighted in official reports.
- Receives binding statutory attention such as (sanctions, reporting mandates, new rights and restrictions)
- Generates sustained debate in Congress, the media, and/or among NGOs.

Negative human-rights law

Not all human rights relevant statutes protect human rights. For example, the Laken Riley Act, is argued by many that it erodes due-process and non-discrimination values while portrayed as public-safety or justice measures[25]. This book treats these as part of the "human-rights discourse," precisely because these reveal whose rights matter the most and whose may be neglected.

Hierarchy of victims

By comparing which communities and countries receive strong legal backing (Uyghurs, Hong Kong activists, Tibetans, Epstein victims) and which do not (Yemeni civilians under coalition bombing, migrants at the U.S. border, dissidents in allied states), we can trace a de facto hierarchy of victims embedded within U.S. law and policies.

Instrumentalization vs. commitment

In a handful of cases, human-rights discourse appears as an instrument for large strategic goals, containment of China, isolation of Iran, justification for sanctions in Venezuela. In other cases, it does reflect more consistent engagement, as with long-term anti-trafficking efforts or genocide prevention standards. Acknowledging these patterns is critical to evaluating "The State of Modern-Day Human Rights."

Roadmap of the Chapters Ahead

With these mechanisms in place, the rest of the book will analyze more concrete cases and statutes:

Part I (Trump I) dissects the laws of the first term:

- Women, Peace, and Security and atrocity prevention.
- North Korea as an example of how far sanctions can stand in for real protection.
- China's Hong Kong, Xinjiang, and Tibet as examples of human rights-driven great power competition.
- Trafficking and "modern day slavery" as bipartisan moralistic aims.

Part II (Trump II) moves within U.S. borders:

- The Laken Riley Act as a case study in "negative human-rights law" and the criminalization of migration.
- The Epstein Files Transparency Act as a rare example where bipartisan pressure forces a nation-state to open its own files in response to sexual exploitation and elite impunity: the reinterpretation and extension of first-term laws—like the Uyghur Act and Caesar Act—to see whether commitments deepen, erode, or simply shift regions.

By the end of this journey, "the state of modern-day human rights" will look less like a universal measurement and more like a guide drawn by Congress, written by the State Department, ingredients from CIA reporting, and selective redraw by two Trump administrations according to their own political, ideological, and strategic priorities. That contested guide is an intense look into the meanings drawn from this book.

Chapter Notes

[1] U.S. Congress. (2017). Women, Peace, and Security Act of 2017 (Public Law 115–68).

[2] Elie Wiesel Genocide and Atrocities Prevention Act of 2018, 2018

[8] Frederick Douglass Trafficking Victims Prevention and Protection Reauthorization Act of 2018, 2018, U.S. Department of Justice, 2023

[9] Congressional Budget Office, 2025

[10] Laken Riley Act, 2025

[11] Epstein Files Transparency Act, 2025

[12] H.R. 4405

[13] National Immigration Law Center. (2025, January 24). Know your rights: Expedited removal expansion.

[15] Hong Kong Human Rights and Democracy Act of 2019, 2019

[17] Elie Wiesel Genocide and Atrocities Prevention Act of 2018, 2018

[19] U.S. Department of State, 2020

[20] U.S. Department of State, 2020

[21] Frederick Douglass Trafficking Victims Prevention and Protection Reauthorization Act of 2018, 2018

[23] U.S. Department of State, 2020

[24] Women, Peace, and Security Act of 2017, 2017. Reuters, 2025

[25] Laken Riley Act, 2025

Chapter 2: Women, Peace, and Security and Atrocity Prevention Frameworks

In chapter 1 I mapped the broad structuring of Trump-era human-rights laws: how Congress, the State Department, the intelligence community, and the White House work together to define which human rights issues gain "legislative traction." This chapter narrows in on two of arguably the most important frameworks from Trump's first term that continue shaping policy in the second: the Women, Peace, and Security (WPS) Act of 2017 and the Elie Wiesel Genocide and Atrocities Prevention Act of 2018[3]. Both important laws were enacted with bipartisan support and signed by President Trump. Both require the executive branch to build cross-agency strategies, conduct training, and report regularly to Congress. Both intersect with national security and human rights, while seeking to translate long-standing normative agendas—such as the U.N. Women, Peace and Security resolutions and international atrocity-prevention norms—into U.S. statute and practice[1]. This chapter describes what these two laws have accomplished, how they were implemented under the first Trump administration, and how they are being understood under the second. I aim to offer a meaningful account of their design, accomplishments, and limits, drawing on official U.S. documents and outside assessments rather than any partisan commentary.

The Women, Peace, and Security Act in Context

Origins in the Global WPS Agenda

- The Women, Peace and Security agenda began with the United Nations system labeled initially the Security Council Resolution 1325[9] while subsequent resolutions emphasized women's participation in peace processes, protection from conflict-related violence, and more specific roles in a post-conflict recovery[8]. The United States adopted its first National Action Plan on Women, Peace, and Security (NAP) in 2011 which was updated in 2016, showing commitment while it integrated the gender perspective into diplomacy, defense, development, and humanitarian policy[7]. The Women, Peace, and Security Act of 2017 was the first U.S. statute to codify this agenda in law. Passed with broad bipartisan support and signed by President Trump on October 6, 2017, the Act expressed the Congress's view that the United States will and should be a global leader in promoting women's participation in conflict prevention and resolution and that women's political participation contributes to more stable societies[5].

What the WPS Act Requires

The WPS Act does not determine new criminal offenses or sanctions. Rather it established policy and planning requirements. Among these provisions, it also highlighted:

- U.S. policy to promote the meaningful participation of women in efforts to prevent, mitigate, and resolve violent conflict and to provide post-conflict relief and recovery[10].
- The Requirement that President to submit and publish a government-wide strategy on Women, Peace, and Security within one year of enactment and again at least every four years[11].
- Mandates that key departments—State, Defense, USAID, and the Department of Homeland Security—develop agency-specific implementation plans consistent with the national strategy[12].
- Calls for training relevant important personnel on the WPS agenda, including how women's participation and protection are linked to U.S. security interests[14]. These provisions illustrate the "framework" law described in Chapter 1: rather than imposition of sanctions, this Act creates more of a structure of strategies, plans, and training obligations that should be actively implemented or possibly unfulfilled minimally with, which might depend on current priorities of the administration leading America.

Implementing WPS under the First Trump Administration

The 2019 U.S. Strategy on Women, Peace, and Security

In June 2019, the White House released the United States Strategy on Women, Peace, and Security, fulfilling the Act's requirement to produce a government-wide strategy[17]. The strategy superseded the earlier NAP and identified three broad objectives: Women are more prepared and increasingly able to participate in efforts that promote stable and lasting peace. Women and girls are safer, better protected, and have equal access to government and private assistance programs. The United States and our partner governments have an improved institutionalization and capacity to ensure WPS efforts are sustainable[16]. A supplement entitled "Metrics and Milestones" document was introduced that set out real goals and indicators—i.e. numbers of personnel trained about WPS, number of women participating in security programs, and the integration of gender analysis into planning documents[15]. These documents have shown that, the first Trump administrations goal was aligned with the notion requiring operationalization of WPS in measurable, interagency terms.

Departmental Implementation Plans

Individual US departments responded with another implementation framework. The Department of Defense issued a Women, Peace, and Security Strategic Framework and Implementation Plan in 2020, outlining additional defense-specific objectives including integrating gender perspectives into military planning, improving women's participation in partner-force training, and developing metrics to track progress[22]. The State Department, USAID, and DHS each published separate plans for integrating WPS into important objectives like diplomacy, development programming, and border/security activities[20]. Furthermore, evaluations by civil society organizations generally acknowledged that these plans marked a step toward institutionalization, while noting that implementation depended very heavily on the leadership, available funding, and staff capacity within each agency[19]. Several analysts further pointed out early metrics tend to focus on quantitative outputs (such as numbers trained) rather than qualitative impacts on women's security or participation in specific conflict settings[18].

Assessment of WPS under Trump I

Based on my observations, three points are clear:

Legal continuity and strategic follow-through.

Under the Trump administration he not only signed the WPS Act but also produced the required strategy and agency plans on schedule, suggesting dedicated institutional buy in at the planning level[23].

Implementation variability

While some bureaus and commands integrated WPS into training and planning, implementation was different by region and specific mission. Publicly available metrics emphasize specific activities (trainings, workshops, policy documents) rather than measurable outcomes, thus making it difficult to assess consistent field-level change[25].

Foundation for later debates

Because WPS was codified in statute and embedded through strategies and plans, it remained a legal requirement even as political rhetoric about gender and security became more polarized in later years[26].

The Elie Wiesel Genocide and Atrocities Prevention Act

Codifying Atrocity Prevention as U.S. Policy

The Elie Wiesel Genocide and Atrocities Prevention Act of 2018 was signed into law by President Trump in January 2019, making the United States one of the first countries to adopt dedicated legislation on preventing mass atrocities[28]. The Act builds on earlier executive initiatives, such as the Atrocities Prevention Board established under President Obama, but now it gives atrocity prevention a clear statutory basis. Among key provisions, the Act:

- Declares that it is U.S. policy to identify, prevent, and respond to the risk of genocide and other mass atrocities[30].
- Requires the President to submit annual reports to Congress on U.S. efforts to prevent and respond to mass atrocities, including descriptions of training programs, and early warning efforts.

The Elie Wiesel Genocide and Atrocities Prevention Act of 2018 was signed into law by President Trump in January 2019, making the United States one of the first countries to adopt dedicated legislation on preventing mass atrocities[31]. The Act builds on earlier executive initiatives, such as the Atrocities Prevention Board established under President Obama, but now it gives atrocity prevention a clear statutory basis.

Among key provisions, the Act:

Declares that it is U.S. policy to identify, prevent, and respond to the risk of genocide and other mass atrocities[38]. Requires the President to submit annual reports to Congress on U.S. efforts to prevent and respond to mass atrocities, including descriptions of training programs, early warning efforts, and use of diplomatic, financial, and other tools[36]. Mandates training for Foreign Service officers and other relevant officials on atrocity-risk factors, early warning, and response options[34]. Encourages enhanced interagency coordination, often carried out through an Atrocity Early Warning Task Force that draws on intelligence and diplomatic reporting[33]. As with the WPS Act, the Elie Wiesel Act institutionalizes existing processes and expectations rather than introduce specific concise policy outcomes in particular crises.

Early Implementation under Trump I

Atrocity Prevention Across Administrations

Continuity into Later Strategies

The atrocity-prevention framework established under the Elie Wiesel Act has been moved forward by multiple administrations. In 2022, the U.S. government released a Strategy to Anticipate, Prevent, and Respond to Atrocities, explicitly citing the Elie Wiesel Act as a foundation and reaffirming atrocity prevention as an enduring policy priority[47]. Additional reporting to Congress in 2023 and in 2024 further underlined ongoing effort to integrate atrocity prevention into regional policy process, early warning systems, and engagement with multilateral partners[45]. Under the second Trump administration, the statutory requirements of the Elie Wiesel Act remain in force. Key analysts note that the administration is again required to submit annual reports and maintain atrocity-prevention coordination mechanisms, thus raising questions about how these obligations might interact with other foreign-policy priorities and resourcing decisions[43].

Observations on Practice

From this vantage point, several observations can be made about atrocity prevention across administrations: Institutionalization vs. discretion. The Elie Wiesel Act firmly establishes atrocity prevention as a U.S. priority at the level of statute and strategy, but decisions about how to act in crises remains highly discretionary. The same legal framework can underlie robust use of sanctions and diplomacy in one context and more limited engagement in another[48]. Could or should this be alarming?

Overlapping with other policy goals.

Atrocity-prevention effort may often coincide with other political objectives and policies—counterterrorism, great-powers competition, and ally management—making it difficult to narrow the field when a measure is primarily "about" human rights and when it is driven by other strategic concerns[50].

Role of reporting and civil society oversight

The Act's annual reporting requirement has created a recurring moment when civil-society organizations and Congress can evaluate progress and press for adjustments, even if they disagree about policy choices in specific countries[52]. This is ideally a great situation for society and non-state actors to have a say in what Congress should or should not do.

WPS and Atrocity Prevention: Converging Frameworks

Although the WPS Act and the Elie Wiesel Act emerged from different advocacy communities, they share several structured features that clarify and are important to understanding "the state of modern-day human rights":

Interagency coordination

Both require coordinated strategies, and implementation plans involving multiple departments and agencies. In practice, mechanisms such as the Atrocity Early Warning Task Force, WPS interagency working groups, and department-level coordinators often rely on similar analytic and planning tools[54]. This proposes much overlap which may or may not hinder the quickness of available decision making.

Training mandates

Both laws emphasize training officials to recognize specific patterns—either gendered impacts of conflict or early warning signs of genocide and mass atrocities. Training modules for diplomats, military officers, and development professionals often integrate WPS and atrocity-prevention content, reinforcing the idea that gender dynamics and mass-violence risks are inherently linked[58]. Reliance on existing tools. Neither law has created an entirely new enforcement mechanism process. Instead, they indicate which and how existing tools—sanctions, visa restrictions, security-sector assistance, public diplomacy—should be used and assessed. This means WPS and atrocity-prevention priorities could be elevated or downplayed without changing the underlying legal authorities[56].This seems like an important built in mechanism to change strategies if necessary.

Metrics and reporting

Both frameworks depend on reporting to Congress and the public. WPS implementation plans include metrics for training and participation; atrocity-prevention reports describe risk assessments and policy responses. Over time, these reports contribute to a data trail that scholars and advocates can analyze, even if there is a competing difference on how to interpret multiple reports and results[60]. Again, strong alignment with a true democratic process. These convergences position WPS and atrocity prevention as invaluable cornerstone frameworks within a very broad human-rights discourse I described in Chapter I, in particular on the foreign-policy side.

Developments under the Second Trump Administration

Ongoing Legal Obligations

The legal obligations created by the WPS Act and the Elie Wiesel Act continue into the second Trump administration. The requirement to maintain a WPS strategy and agency implementation plans remains in force, as do training and reporting duties[64]. Similarly, atrocity-prevention reporting and coordination obligations remain binding under the Elie Wiesel Act[62]. Trump II administration has inherited a significant amount of human-rights framework that are very difficult to ignore, even if the administration chooses to reinterpret them, adjust funding, or shift its emphasis among numerous policy tools.

The WPS Debate at the Pentagon

One prominent example of how statutory frameworks can be interpreted differently is the recent debate over WPS within the Department of Defense. In April 2025, Defense Secretary Pete Hegseth announced the termination of the Pentagon's dedicated Women, Peace and Security program, describing it as a "woke" initiative and stating that the department would comply only with minimum legal requirements[69]. Reports indicate that the decision generated much criticism from both Democratic and Republican lawmakers who had supported the WPS Act and from some current and former security officials who viewed WPS as aligned with U.S. strategic interests[67]. The State Department has reiterated its intention to continue implementing WPS obligations in its own portfolio[66]. Hegseth's policy shift in this episode further illustrates how implementation of the same exact statute can vary significantly and does across agencies and over time, even when the underlying legal framework remains unchanged. It also underscores the role of Congress and civil society in monitoring compliance and debating the appropriate scope of WPS initiatives.

Atrocity Prevention in a Changing Strategic Environment

Atrocity-prevention policy under Trump II is still being created. Existing analyses have emphasized that the administration is required to continue reporting under the Elie Wiesel Act and that atrocity-prevention considerations intersect with ongoing debates about U.S. priorities in regions such as the Middle East, Eastern Europe, and Africa[74]. Observers note two key questions that will be explored in later chapters: How consistently will atrocity-prevention analysis be integrated into high-level decisions? What will be the implications? The statutory framework has clearly provided the tools and expectations, but the degree to which those tools are decisive in policymaking can vary decisively[72]. How will atrocity prevention interact with other agendas, including great-power competition and migration control? As Chapter 1 noted, human-rights framework can at times reinforce broader strategic goals and sit in tension with them. Atrocity-prevention mandates may be interpreted differently when they align with other priorities than when they appear to constrain them[71]. From a structured perspective, however, the key contribution is to acknowledge that the Elie Wiesel Act has created a durable channel: annual reports, defined interagency processes, and training through which atrocity-prevention considerations continue to surface, regardless of administration.

Human Rights: What This Reveals About Modern Day Human Rights

Taken together, the WPS Act and the Elie Wiesel Act have highlighted several features of the "modern-day human-rights system" as it currently operates in U.S. policy. Firstly, human-rights concerns can be embedded in security policy through framework legislation. Both laws explicitly link values (gender equality, protection from mass atrocities) to U.S. national interests, arguing that societies where women participate and mass violence is prevented are more stable partners[80]. Arguably a milestone for human rights legislature in the modern era. Secondly, these remarkable initiatives illustrate the tension between continuity and discretion. The legal framework and strategies have remained in place across administrations, but measurable practical impact depends on how far executive officials choose to go beyond minimum compliance, how much funding is allocated, and how strongly Congress and civil society press for robust implementation[78]. Thirdly, they provide clarity to the significant importance of reporting and metrics in modern human-rights governance and responsibilities. Regular reports to Congress on WPS and atrocity prevention has created a public record of activities, priorities, and self-identified gaps. Even when these documents are mostly cautious in tone, they provide material for outside analysis and debate, as well as offer a baseline for evaluating changes over time[76]. Finally, these human rights initiatives demonstrate that the state of modern-day human rights is not determined solely by high-profile crises or sanctions laws. It is also shaped by less visible infrastructure—strategies, training curricula, interagency task forces that influence how officials perceive risks, plan operations, and weigh the human-rights consequences with more broad policy choices.

Looking Ahead

The next chapters will move from frameworks to country-specific applications, examining how WPS and atrocity-prevention considerations intersected with U.S. responses in particular contexts during the Trump years. Case studies will include Xinjiang, where the Uyghur Human Rights Policy Act, atrocity-prevention analysis, and great-power competition each overlapped. Selected Middle Eastern contexts where WPS and atrocity-prevention tools were invoked in security-sector assistance as well as peacekeeping. By monitoring how these tools were used or not used in specific situations, the book will test whether the components described in Chapters 1 and 2 have translated into meaningful protection on the ground, and how that should and will be more informative within future debates about the role of human rights in U.S. foreign policy.

As with the WPS Act, the Elie Wiesel Act institutionalizes existing processes and expectations rather than introduce specific concise policy outcomes in particular crises.

Chapter Notes

[1] S.1141—Women, Peace, and Security Act of 2017, 2017

[3] U.S. Congress. (2017). Women, Peace, and Security Act of 2017 (Public Law 115–68).

[5] S.1141—Women, Peace, and Security Act of 2017, 2017

[7] U.S. National Action Plan on Women, Peace, and Security, 2024

[8] U.S. National Action Plan on Women, Peace, and Security, 2024

[9] 2000

[10] U.S. Congress. (2017). Women, Peace, and Security Act of 2017 (Public Law 115–68).

[11] Women, Peace, and Security Strategy, 2019

[12] U.S. Congress. (2017). Women, Peace, and Security Act of 2017 (Public Law 115–68).

[14] S.1141—Women, Peace, and Security Act of 2017, 2017

[15] Women, Peace, and Security Strategy: Milestones & Metrics, 2019

[16] From the Trump to the Biden Administration: The Women, Peace and Security Agenda, 2022

[17] United States Strategy on Women, Peace, and Security, 2019

[18] From the Trump to the Biden Administration: The Women, Peace and Security Agenda, 2022

[19] A Decade in Review: The Women, Peace and Security Agenda, 2022

[20] Women, Peace, and Security—State Department, 2024

[22] Department of Defense WPS Strategic Framework, 2020

[23] United States Strategy on Women, Peace, and Security, 2019

[25] A Decade in Review: The Women, Peace and Security Agenda, 2022

[26] U.S. Congress. (2017). Women, Peace, and Security Act of 2017 (Public Law 115–68).

[28] Elie Wiesel Genocide and Atrocities Prevention Act of 2018, Pub. L. No. 115-441, 132 Stat. 5586 (2019).

[30] S.1158—Elie Wiesel Genocide and Atrocities Prevention Act of 2018, 2018

[31] Elie Wiesel Genocide and Atrocities Prevention Act of 2018, Pub. L. No. 115-441, 132 Stat. 5586 (2019).

[33] 2025 Mass Atrocities Policy Update, 2025

[34] Elie Wiesel Genocide and Atrocities Prevention Act of 2018, Pub. L. No. 115-441, 132 Stat. 5586 (2019).

[36] S.1158—Elie Wiesel Genocide and Atrocities Prevention Act of 2018, 2018

[38] S.1158—Elie Wiesel Genocide and Atrocities Prevention Act of 2018, 2018

[43] What the White House and Congress Can Do to Prevent Mass Atrocities, 2025

[45] 2023 Report to Congress on Section 5, 2023

[47] New U.S. Atrocity Prevention Strategy, 2022

[48] Elie Wiesel Genocide and Atrocities Prevention Act of 2018, Pub. L. No. 115-441, 132 Stat. 5586 (2019).

[50] New U.S. Atrocity Prevention Strategy, 2022

[52] PPWG Assessment of 2020 Elie Wiesel Report, 2020

[54] 2025 Mass Atrocities Policy Update, 2025

[58] Elie Wiesel Genocide and Atrocities Prevention Report, 2019

[60] Women, Peace, and Security Strategy: Milestones & Metrics, 2019

[62] 2024 Report to Congress on Section 5, 2024

[64] U.S. Congress. (2017). Women, Peace, and Security Act of 2017 (Public Law 115–68).

[66] Women, Peace, and Security—State Department, 2024

[67] Hegseth Scraps Pentagon's Women, Peace and Security Program, 2025

[69] Pentagon Chief Cancels Program on Women in Security, 2025

[71] What the White House and Congress Can Do to Prevent Mass Atrocities, 2025

[72] New U.S. Atrocity Prevention Strategy, 2022

[74] What the White House and Congress Can Do to Prevent Mass Atrocities, 2025

[76] Women, Peace, and Security Strategy: Milestones & Metrics, 2019

[78] A Decade in Review: The Women, Peace and Security Agenda, 2022

[80] U.S. Congress. (2017). Women, Peace, and Security Act of 2017 (Public Law 115–68).

Chapter 3: Post–Cold War Globalism, Relativism, and the Human-Rights System

When I talk about Trump-era human-rights mechanisms in this book, I am not describing something just recently implemented in 2017. Those statutes and institutions I described in the first two chapters, —the WPS Act, the Elie Wiesel Act, sanctions laws, country reports, atrocity prevention task forces are merely layered atop of much older global concepts that began to shape up further post-Cold -War and gained significant momentum since. This chapter will step back from Washington's definitions to look at the enormous scope and further investigate the enhancements.

I focus on three tangled questions:

- How did the international and U.S. human-rights system evolve after the Cold War?
- What do I mean by "globalism" in this book, and why does it matter?
- How have the different U.S. administrations—ending with Trump I and Trump II position themselves toward a globalized system?

NGOs and advocacy networks are an intricate part to these evolvements, but I will provide more detailed scrutiny of their roles in later, case- study based chapters where their influence becomes critical. In the first chapter I outlined the fundamentals of the Trump-era human-rights theory: Congress is lawmaker and overseer; the State Department as narrator-in-chief; the intelligence community as stealth reporter, and the presidency as gatekeeper and signal generator. In chapter 2 I narrowed in on two framework statutes—the Women, Peace, and Security Act of 2017 and the Elie Wiesel Genocide and Atrocities Prevention Act of 2018—and showed how they codified gender and atrocity-prevention agendas within U.S. law. What those chapters hinted at is that none of these can operate in complete isolation. They interact frequently with: UN human-rights organizations and regional courts long-standing treaties, global discourse of "universal human rights," as well as increasingly, populist and sovereignty-based pushback against "globalists" and "foreign judges." Trump's first and second administrations tend to function less as a leave of absence but more as an examination of institutions and discourse established over decades. To understand "the state of modern-day human rights," we need to know what exactly the discourse is: which assumptions about universality are in the discourse, which institutions, and what are if, very few of, the shared expectations about how nation-states should treat their citizens.

UN and treaty-based mechanisms

The legal backbone of the global human-rights regime is familiar: the Universal Declaration of Human Rights[1] and the two major covenants on civil and political rights and on economic, social, and cultural rights. But it was after the Cold War that the accompanying institutions became more relevant at the same time and much more routine. By the 1990s and 2000s, nine significant UN human-rights treaties had functioning monitoring committees ("treaty bodies") with examined state reports, issued concluding observations, and, in some cases, considered individual complaints (for example under the ICCPR Optional Protocol). These committees are not courts but do produce a stream of legal interpretation and public and societal pressures: these define recognition of torture, discrimination, arbitrary detention, or due-process violations in concise and specific ways. Alongside these treaty bodies, the United Nations constructed new "special procedures" including independent experts referred to as Special Rapporteurs on torture, freedom of expression, violence against women, or specific countries. Each has specific roles to investigate, to conduct country visits, issue reports, and send urgent communications to governments, which help to form a flexible early-warning and an identification system to themes and crises. In 2006, when the Human Rights Council replaced the Commission on Human Rights, the UN also introduced the Universal Periodic Review (UPR). Every member state will now undergo a peer review of its human-rights record approximately every 4.5 years. These are based on national reports, UN information, and stakeholder submissions. Despite shortcomings, the UPR has been intended to define the notion that human-rights performance is something states should discuss in a structured, reoccurring way and not be confined to "crisis" situations. For this book, my point is simple: by the time Trump enters office, "international human rights" are not limited to specific declarations or sets of treaties. Instead, they represent a conglomeration of rights committees, rapporteurs, reviews, and reporting cycles that do create specific expectations, refined vocabulary, and renewed evidence positions that U.S. policymakers both rely upon and may also resist.

Regional systems

In contrast; more regional human-rights systems have intensified. The European Court of Human Rights has long issued binding judgments on important issues such as police abuse, to media freedoms. The Inter-American Court and Commission and the African Commission and Court have provided similar, yet less enforced, regional oversight. These rights bodies are important to U.S. debates in at least two ways: They generate examples of the legal reasoning that advocates and officials in Washington may refer to: rulings on torture, fair trials, and discrimination. They show that rights litigation and accountability do not just appear within the UN; but they are visible in regional and domestic courts, thus reinforcing the idea that human-rights violations are subject to litigation, and not solely political measures.

The United States inside this evolving system

The U.S. has helped create much of this trajectory, from the post–World War II moments and ongoing. During the late Cold War, human rights discourse was often blended with anti-communism, supporting dissidents in the Soviet bloc while ignoring some abuses by anti-communist allies. After 1989, however, this "universal rights" story gained new momentum, the new end of ideological rivalry seemed to open space for an integrated human-rights theory, including newly formed tribunals for Yugoslavia and Rwanda, and, eventually, the International Criminal Court. Washington's relationship to this expanding regime has always been reserved. However, it has promoted and supported some institutions and theories (civil and political rights, democracy, and the prohibition of genocide and torture). It has resisted or selectively engaged with others (for example, the ICC, some economic and social rights, and certain treaty obligations). But the key point for this book is that by the early 21st century, U.S. human-rights policy no longer operates alone. Statutes like the WPS Act or the Elie Wiesel Act coexist and further the existing conglomeration of several global theories and institutions, even though some U.S. leaders criticize and partially withdraw from some.

The word "globalism" has become a political insult in some positions, especially in the Trump-era rhetoric. Here, I use it in an analytical sense referring to three intertwined developments that shape modern human-rights politics:

Economic globalism

The integration of markets through trade, finance, and supply chains. Institutional/legal globalism – the spread of international organizations, treaties, and courts, including the human-rights institutions described above.

Normative globalism

The idea that a shared "world culture" is recognized as more appropriate state behavior, including human rights, democracy, and rule of law, which some scholars call "world polity." Globalism is not a conspiracy; it is definitive of numerous patterns of dependence globally between nation-states and shared standards that make it possible, for example, for a torture allegation in one country to show up in UN reporting, then in a congressional hearing, then in a sanction's designation meeting. This globalism matters differently to different state actors: Major powers can benefit from institutional rules and markets they authored but may also fear these constraints on their freedom of action and sovereignty. Many governments in the Global South see the human-rights empire as both a protection source and a potential instrument of political pressure. International organizations rely on universalist claims to maintain legitimacy. Populist and nationalist movements often portray these "globalists" as elite threats to national sovereignty. Trump-era politicism now coincides inside this. This administration has used sanctions and human-rights language against rival states, yet meantime they are accused of attacking or bypassing the multilateral institutions and legal norms that made these mechanisms a reality.

Universalism in practice, not just on paper

The post–Cold War consolidation of treaties and institutions rested on a universalist claim that there are some rights every person holds simply by being human, regardless of nationality, culture, or religion. UN offices routinely describe universality as a core principle that human beings are "endowed with equal human rights simply by virtue of being human, wherever they live and whoever they are." Legal universalism does not mean uniform recognition or practice. The Geneva Academy, for example, indicates that human rights are legally universal but unevenly realized in a world still marked by poverty, discrimination, conflict, and authoritarian rule. Part of the human-rights project since the 1990s has involved trying to close this gap, through monitoring, litigation, and policy reform.

Cultural relativism and "Asian values"

From the early 1990s, another parallel discourse argued and insisted that universalism mirrored a Western liberal agenda. In the "Asian values" debate, leaders in parts of East and Southeast Asia have claimed that their societies prioritize harmony, hierarchy, community, and economic development over individual rights or adversarial politics, and that human-rights concepts should be interpreted through these local values. Similar claims have been made in Islamic, African, and other contexts, where many governments claim that these westernized international standards on women's rights, LGBTQ+ rights, religious freedom, or free expression, clash directly with their religious laws and cultural traditions. Cultural relativism can operate on numerous levels:

As a philosophical critique: can there be a single, global standard of rights?

As a political tactic appealing to "tradition" or "civilizational difference" to deflect criticism of specific laws or practice, and as a negotiating posture which demands more flexibility in how universal rights should be applied. For the purposes of this book, what matters more is not resolving the philosophical dispute, but learning how a relativist argument can shape real outcomes and when they succeed in avoiding criticism, as well as when universalist claims seemingly prevail.

Populist anti-globalism and sovereignty

In the 2010s and 2020s, a different kind of response became apparent not from primary cultural arguments but from populist, nationalist projects. "Globalism" in this sense has become a negative label for the perceived transnational elite, bureaucrats, judges, NGOs, and corporate actors who are often accused of undermining the will or rights of "the people." Some critics say Trump's rhetoric is an illuminating example. He has indicated "the future" as belonging to patriots, not globalists, and cast multilateral institution from the UN to trade bodies as hindering U.S. sovereignty and prosperity claiming international courts and human-rights bodies can't be trusted because they are unelected and foreign related. Transnational commitments (on refugees, climate, or racial equality) are recast as threats to national identity and security. Domestic reforms that were justified in human-rights language (for example, diversity or non-discrimination programs) are attacked as partisan or "woke." Anti-globalism and cultural relativism do overlap in some situations and separate within others. Both, however, challenge the idea that there is a shared, stable set of human-rights norms that can contain what sovereign governments can do.

Against this background, Trump I and Trump II can be understood as one phase in a long U.S. history, rather than total breakdown.

Late Cold War and the 1990s

During the late Cold War, U.S. human-rights rhetoric was intertwined with geopolitical competition. Dissidents in the Soviet bloc, had become a symbol of a much wider struggle between "freedoms" and "communism," even as some anti-communist allies' abuses attracted less attention. In the 1990s, the mood shifted toward what some described as liberal internationalism. International criminal tribunals for Yugoslavia and Rwanda signaled a stronger commitment to accountability for atrocities. NATO interventions in Bosnia and Kosovo were justified partly in human-rights and humanitarian terms, laying groundwork for the later "Responsibility to Protect" (R2P) doctrine. Democracy and human rights became more explicit conditions in some aid and trade agreements. Human-rights discourse in this period expanded, and the U.S. cast itself as heroic even when its own practices (for example on the death penalty or social rights) did not exactly match the rhetoric.

2000s: War on Terror and selective universality

The 2000s complicated the entire picture. The Bush administration often spoke in universal terms about freedom and democracy, particularly in the Middle East, while simultaneously pursuing counterterrorism policies including indefinite detention, (Guantanamo Bay) extraordinary rendition, and coercive interrogation that many UN bodies and NGOs labeled as human-rights violations. This period showed how a state could affirm universal human rights rhetorically, promote them externally (for example, funding democracy programs), and then contest or reinterpret them when they constrained their own security policies.

Obama: engagement and institutionalization

The Obama administration sought to re-engage with multilateral institutions, signaling support for the Human Rights Council and various UN initiatives, while launching the Atrocities Prevention Board in 2012 leading framework to the later Elie Wiesel Act. At the same time, his administration-maintained elements of the previous counterterrorism architecture, including targeted killings and surveillance programs. The result was deepening of atrocity-prevention and WPS agendas, and in no way a departure from earlier security practices.

Trump I: America First in a globalist system

By the time Trump takes office in his first term, there is a list that he inherits which included a massive set of global networks and human-rights institutions, existing U.S. commitments to atrocity prevention, and the WPS which is a domestic system in which Congress has codified sanctions, human-rights reporting, and trafficking policies. Trump I marked a shift in choices: which included withdrawal from the UN Human Rights Council and sharp rhetoric against "globalists" and multilateral bodies. In addition, more confrontational use of human-rights discourse and sanctions against certain political rivals: (China over Xinjiang, Venezuela, Iran, North Korea). A de-emphasis on human rights in relations with some authoritarian partners, positioning around security, migration control, and some business interests. At the same time, as Chapters 1 and 2 have shown, Trump I did sign bipartisan human-rights laws: the WPS Act, the Elie Wiesel Act, several country-specific acts, and trafficking-related reauthorizations. That mix of anti-globalist rhetoric and continued use of rights-based instruments actually makes the period analytically interesting.

Trump II: Intensifying the rhetoric

Trump's return to office in 2025 has deepened the discourse. International observers, including the UN High Commissioner for Human Rights and Amnesty International, have described a "fundamental shift" in the U.S. approach to human rights and a broader "freefall of rights" globally linked to Trump's policies. Noteworthy signs of this shifting have included: Further disengagement from UN human-rights processes, such as failing to attend a scheduled Universal Periodic Review session and signaling reluctance to submit national reports. Domestic moves that roll back equity and anti-discrimination programs, considered as opposition to "woke" agendas rather than retreats from rights commitments. At the same time, the statutory obligations created by Congress including WPS and Elie Wiesel requirement still remain as law. As earlier chapters described, Trump II has begun to reinterpret and perhaps minimize some of these obligations in certain agencies while still using sanction-based laws and human-rights rhetoric in selected foreign-policy situations. Summarily, Trump II administration does not abolish the human rights discourse, it operates within it, reallocating attention, resources, and legitimacy in ways that remain to be seen.

Stepping back from these findings, three conclusions come to the top in the remainder of this book. First, the contemporary human-rights system is deeply intertwined with globalism in the analysis context. Additionally, the existence of thorough treaties and institutions, the western normative expectations of

universality, and the cross-border flow of information and scrutiny. This does not depend on any one administration, but a major world power like the United States can strengthen these or weaken them through participation, funding, and leadership examples. Second, cultural relativism and populist anti-globalism have provided powerful language of renowned resistance. They allow governments and certain movements an argument that several human-rights demands are foreign, partisan, elitist, or culturally inappropriate. In practice, these arguments do not totally reject human rights; they contest which rights, for whom, and under whose interpretive authority. Third, Trump I and Trump II should be interpreted not as a simple "break" and more as a renewed interpretation of this. They now show how far a major state actor can push sovereignty and anti-globalist rhetoric while using human-rights tools and discourse in dealings with others.
Furthermore, just how much statutory frameworks (like WPS and atrocity-prevention laws) inhibit or provide executive discretion, even when the executive is skeptical of the broader global sense, and how quickly perceptions of U.S. leadership or deflection can shift in the eyes of UN officials, other governments, and rights observers. The chapters that follow return to more rights terrain: specific countries, laws, and controversies—including Venezuela, Xinjiang, and migration detention. In each case, I will ask how the post–Cold War rights discourse, this contested globalism, and these Trump-era decisions combine in practice and ask who will gain protections, who will be left out, and what that can clear up about the state of modern-day human rights.

Chapter Notes [1] 1948

Chapter 4: Venezuela: Repression, Sanctions, and the Limits of Protection

In the previous chapter, I transitioned from Trump-era statutes and pivoted back to intricate global implications: the post–Cold War expansion of human-rights institutions, the additional and competing idea and criticisms about the debated concept of "globalism," and the way Trump I and Trump II administrations have acted within this seemingly very diverse system. I concluded by promising that the next chapters would move to more concise case studies: specific countries, laws, and new controversies such as the now highly visible Venezuela, Xinjiang, and migration detention, and then ponder who is getting human rights protections and who isn't. Venezuela seemed like a logical place to narrate, in recognition of a combination of all three issues: A frightfully and alarming internal human-rights specific as well as humanitarian crisis. A diversified combination of international response from UN fact-finding and the International Criminal Court (ICC) to regional organizations, as well as NGOs. A U.S. role that has shifted from a more liberal internationalism viewpoint "maximum pressure," and even now to a more militarized, sovereignty-asserting posturing under Trump II.[1] 2020, 2023) The Venezuelan case proposes an interesting inquiry. When a state is both repressing its population and fiercely defending its sovereignty, what should the contemporary human-rights system consider implementing? And how does the U.S. policy discourse around human-rights language shaped by sanctions, migration fears, and geopolitics respond within this complicated picture?

Several features make Venezuela a promising first case study for this book and analysis, First the sheer size and length of this crisis. Over the past decade, state repression, economic mismanagement, and political conflict have directly created one of the world's most contemporary largest displacement crises, while millions of Venezuelans have left the country and those who remain face severe shortages, collapsed public services, and systemic violations of civil and political rights.[5] Second, the intricacy of international involvement. Venezuela is not an overlooked crisis; it is the subject of regular UN Human Rights Council debates, repeated reports by an Independent International Fact-Finding Mission, ICC examinations, regional diplomacy in the Americas, and a considerable amount of NGO advocacy. Third, the country has become a strong point for U.S. foreign policy involvement. Washington's response combines sanctions, public reporting, and support for democratic actors with even more posturing and sovereignty-centered discourse that the newest Trump-era policies have demonstrated for the world. Under Trump I, this took the form of escalating economic and financial sanctions; under Trump II, it has moved toward naval strikes, airspace closures, and open discussion of possible military options.[3] Finally, Venezuela captures the human rights discourse first highlighted in Chapter 3: the disagreement between universalist human-rights claims and arguments about national sovereignty; the unrecognized role of major powers in a "globalist" system; and the means by which a populist anti-globalism stance may both weaponize and undermine human-rights discourse.

Patterns of repression

The Venezuelan crisis is not limited to as an economic forum alone. The crises are widely recognized to be a deliberate strategy to eliminate political opposition and social dissent. UN fact-finding missions and NGO reports describe the activities in detail: Arbitrary detentions of opposition figures, activists, and protesters. Reported torture and ill-treatment in detention, especially by intelligence and security services. Excessive use of force in demonstrations and security operations. Politicized prosecutions and restrictions on independent media and civil society. These are not isolated cases of severe human rights abuse activities. They are highly recognized in a large effort to maintain power in the face of extreme electoral challenges and very deep unpopularity. International monitors have described these as systematic with certain reports escalating to levels of crimes against humanity.

Socioeconomic collapse and everyday rights

Venezuelans have faced severe deprivation of their economic and social rights. Even before the U.S. "maximum pressure" sanctions; years of mismanagement, corruption, and dependence on oil revenues have produced hyperinflation, as well as food and medicine shortages. Furthermore, there is strong erosion of public infrastructure. Sanctions and countermeasures have also influenced this preexisting collapse in a complicated manner. Reports by UN bodies and NGOs document widespread food insecurity and child malnutrition, hospital shortages, power outages, and disruptions to clean water. Barriers to basic healthcare and essential medicines. A steep decline in minimum living standards for large parts of the population.[6] This mixture of strong political repression and related socioeconomic collapses have made Venezuela an exemplary example of what it means for a nation-state to be viewed as an "acute human-rights crisis" in the 21st century.

Displacement and regional ripple effects

The human impact is not confined to Venezuela's borders. Millions of Venezuelans have left their country, thus creating one of the largest displacement movements in the modern world. Neighboring states in Latin America have become host to large refugee and migrant settlements and producing a real strain upon services and politics. This regional dimension is very concerning and directly related to the theme of globalism: this crisis is not only about how a government can treat its citizens, but more importantly an example of how cross-border migration of persons, money, oil, and information can generate broader pressures on the human-rights system and on regional stability.[8]

Venezuela is also a case study for the multi-layer mechanisms outlined in Chapter 3: treaty bodies, special procedures, fact-finding missions, regional courts, and the ICC.

UN fact-finding and monitoring

The UN Human Rights Council created an Independent International Fact-Finding Mission on the Bolivarian Republic of Venezuela in 2019. Since then, the Mission has produced detailed reports documenting patterns of extrajudicial killings, arbitrary detention, and torture, and linking them to specific institutions and chains of command. Alongside these, the Office of the UN High Commissioner for Human Rights (OHCHR) has issued periodic reports on the situation and has participated in the technical cooperation with Venezuelan authorities, with mixed access and cooperative responses. The Venezuelan government has responded with an all too familiar mixture of rejection and limited cooperation denouncing allegations as biased and politically motivated and contesting findings. However, at times they do cooperate with OHCHR while pointing to its own reform initiatives as evidence of progress. This is a classic example of how universalist monitoring meets sovereignty-based resistance.

ICC, regional organizations, and NGOs

Beyond the UN: The International Criminal Court has been examining allegations of crimes against humanity in Venezuela, a process that has become symbolic and a legal point for accountability debate. Regional bodies, such as the Organization of American States (OAS), have issued their own reports and resolutions, though they are divided by political fault lines in the hemisphere. NGOs like Human Rights Watch, Amnesty International, and regional organizations have supplied documentation, legal analysis, and advocacy campaigns that feed into UN and ICC processes. The result is this "conglomeration" of human rights systems mentioned in Chapter 3 which include treaty bodies, special procedures, fact-finding missions, courts, and NGOs, all of which are generating a steady stream of narratives, legal arguments, and evidentiary records regarding horrendous Venezuelan human rights abuses. What these mechanisms cannot do unilaterally is force a change in power or immediate policy reversal. They do however create pressure, stigmatize, and add legal risk; but do not provide simple enforcement mechanisms or procedures.

The United States as Actor: From Liberal Internationalism to "Maximum Pressure" and Beyond

Against this complicated background, U.S. policy has shone as both centralized and contested. Furthermore, this further illustrates how a major power may position itself inside and against a "globalist" human-rights system simultaneously.

Before Trump: a brief prelude

Under previous administrations, U.S. policy toward Venezuela combined concern over democratic backsliding and human-rights abuses with more traditional methods, targeted sanctions on specific officials, support for civil society and democratic actors, and rhetorical alignment with multilateral efforts. Human rights were a distinct part of the discourse, but these were only one among numerous real concerns, alongside energy, regional security, and ideologies.

Trump I: "Maximum pressure" and selective solidarity

Trump's first term brought a sharp unilateral edge. In 2017, his administration issued a series of executive orders that expanded upon sanctions from individual officials to broad financial and oil-sector measures, thus restricting Venezuela's access to U.S. capital markets and targeting its state oil company. These steps became justified in terms of human-rights abuses, corruption, and democratic breakdown.[11] Trump I also recognized a rival interim government and called openly for regime change, framing Nicolás Maduro as an illegitimate "dictator," while signaling support for opposition-led protests and regional pressure. Human-rights language remained present, sanctions were issued as tools to defend democracy and punish abuses, but his strategies aligned with more confrontational, sovereignty assertions that Chapter 3 has already identified as examples of Trump-era anti-globalist discourse. His critics argued that broad financial and oil sanctions exacerbated humanitarian suffering and weakened ordinary Venezuelans more than the elites they were meant to target. Reports by think tanks and advocacy organizations have documented how sanctions contributed to economic contraction, complicated imports, and reduced state revenues, even if mismanagement and corruption were already central drivers of the collapse.[9] His supporters of "maximum pressure," emphasized the inherent need to confront a regime implicated in serious human rights abuses and alleged criminal activity, and further argued that inaction would continue to normalize authoritarian rule.

Between Trump I and Trump II

The administration that followed Trump I recalibrated some of these policies, experimenting with partial sanctions relief in exchange for limited political concessions, while maintaining strong discourse and scrutiny of Venezuelan human-rights violations. The broad sanctions, however, remained, further illustrating one of the key points from Chapter 3: once human-rights-based sanctions are codified into domestic law, they can outlive individual presidents and become a semi- permanent feature of foreign policy.

Trump II: Militarization and renewed escalation

Trump's return to office in 2025 has brought a more overtly militarized dimension to the Venezuela story. In addition to re-imposing and tightening sanctions, his administration expanded naval and aerial operations targeting alleged drug-smuggling vessels linked to Venezuela, including strikes that have killed scores of people and raised questions about compliance with international humanitarian law[19] Declared Venezuelan airspace "closed" and used the language of territorial control and self-defense in justifying threats of further action[17] Left open the possibility of direct military intervention, framing it as a last-resort response to narco-terrorism, mass migration, and threats to U.S. security.[15] At the same time, Trump II officials continue to cite human rights with mentions of UN and NGO reports on repression, ICC proceedings, and the Venezuelan government's crackdowns as justification for their stance[13].

The response is attributable yet consistent with the Trump-era mixture of anti-globalist discourse and the readiness to bypass multilateral procedures and combine selective reliance on those same procedures to support that the other side is failing.

Venezuela also represents the ongoing disagreements regarding sanctions as human-rights enforcement methods.

The case for sanctions as protection

Proponents of broad sanctions have argued that they signal that systemic abuses and authoritarian consolidation carry consequences. They inhibit a regime's access to financial, and material resources used to sustain repression. They increase negotiations and political transitions by increased pressure on key actors. Within this viewpoint, the human-rights harm of inaction and allowing a repressive government to consolidate indefinitely, would outweigh the indirect economic harms caused by sanctions. Some U.S. and European policymakers explicitly confirm sanctions as part of an atrocity-prevention and democracy-defense toolkit, aligning with the statutory mechanisms described in Chapter 2.[21]

The case against broad sanctions

Some critics, including humanitarian organizations and select academic analysts would disagree that broad financial and oil sanctions intensify economic crises that are already harming the citizenry, when imposed on an economy heavily dependent upon a single export. Authoritarian elite actors can find ways to redirect limited resources and smuggling revenues, while the poor citizenry is directly affected by shortages, inflation, and collapsing services. Sanctions can be used domestically by the targeted government to reinforce nationalist narratives, blame external enemies, and justify further crackdowns.[24] Within this perspective, sanctions meant to defend human rights and punish those responsible could end up undermining economic and social rights, while doing little to change the political powers of those offenders in power.

Mixed evidence and unintended consequences

The evidence from Venezuela to date is mixed and highly politicized. Sanctions clearly interact with preexisting structural problems, making it difficult to attribute specific outcomes to single causes. Some analysts suggest poor sequence or weak conditional sanctions relief can solidify authoritarian power by injecting new resources without securing lasting reforms. Others argue that long-term maximum pressure without realistic diplomatic offramps entrenches hardliners and reduces leverage.[26] For the purposes of this book, my key point cannot resolve ongoing sanctions debates but does analyze what this reveals about the state of modern-day human rights. Human-rights language is centralized on opposite sides of the confrontation. There is no definitive consensus whether a given set of measures count as a human-rights "solution" or are they part of the problem? The people most affected, ordinary Venezuelan citizens, have little to say about these decisions, which are made in Caracas, Washington, and other capitals.

Reflecting upon the first three chapters, Venezuela brings in countless themes, first, it shows both the reach and the limitations of globalism. On one hand, Venezuelan authorities are entrenched with complex considerations of discourse, and institutions including UN fact-finding missions, ICC examination, regional diplomacy, NGO reporting, and sanctions all justified in the name of human-rights abuse discourse. As a consequence, these actors have been able to maintain power for numerous years despite this pressure, relying on security forces, external partners, and appeals to sovereignty and anti-imperialism. Second, Venezuela demonstrates how universalist and sovereignty-based narratives collide. International actors cite universal human rights and accountability; the Venezuelan government responds with discourse of non-intervention, anti-colonialism, and nationalism. Trump-era policies, with emphasis on national interests, unilateral action, and suspicion of multilateral constraints, add another layer to this important discussion as a major power that partly embraces and partly rejects the "globalist" position. Third, it demonstrates how human-rights discourse can be justified in very different policy choices. Sanctions and military pressure are defended to protect Venezuelans from repression; critics describe them as violations of the same population's economic and social rights. The fact that both claims are made in the language of human rights further the political and arguable nature of contemporary human rights considerations. Fourth, Venezuela reflects the asymmetry of power in the human-rights arena. Venezuelan activists, victims, and migrants rely on international mechanisms for their visibility and possible accountability. However, decisions about sanctions, military deployments, and diplomatic strategy are made by nation-states pursuing calculated and strategic motivations. The result is a system in which those most affected by abuses have very little control over the tools attempting to be implemented on their behalf. Finally, this case study confirms a hypothesis from Chapter 3:

Trump I and Trump II have not abolished human-rights discourse.

They operate solely within it, appropriating UN and NGO findings, using statutory discourse regarding sanctions and atrocity prevention, and invoke the suffering of innocent Venezuelans while at the same time contest multilateral constraint, prioritize sovereignty and security, and push the boundaries of what international law can justify or allow.

Venezuela is one large piece of an enormous puzzle. A huge part of the ongoing question of repression, sanctions, and sovereignty in the Western Hemisphere. The next chapters turn to other test cases such as Xinjiang, and U.S. migration detention that bring different aspects of the same system into view, mass surveillance and re-education in a rising power, the politics of intervention and non-intervention in conflict, and the role of human-rights discourse at and within a nation-state's borders. Across these cases, the prolific questions remain the same: Who can realistically expect protection from the contemporary human-rights system, and under what conditions? Whose suffering becomes legible as a human-rights emergency and whose will remain marginalized? How do global human rights mechanisms and institutions shape, and fail to shape, the choices of powerful nation-states? Venezuela, as the first concrete example, suggests that the answers will not be simply explained. The machinery built after the Cold War is active and very visible; universalist discourse remains strong, yet positive outcomes will depend largely upon on a charged mixture of domestic policies/politics, geopolitical competitions, and two-sided arguments as well as interpretations of what human rights really are in the state of modern-day human rights.

In my previous chapter, Venezuela served as an entry point into this ongoing human-rights discourse analysis: a government presiding over repression and socioeconomic collapse, an active grouping of UN bodies and NGOs documenting closely the abuses, and the United States switching between multilateral discourse and terms of unilateral "maximum pressure." In this next chapter I have turned to a different configuration of state power, Xinjiang in the People's Republic of China. These alleged human rights violations are at least hardline, but the state alleged is a permanent member of the UN Security Council and a central and powerful player of a more newly recognized globalized economy. Now the resulting human-rights departure that doesn't resemble a failing state but does resemble a laboratory of algorithmic authoritarianism. Algorithmic authoritarianism is the use of automated systems and data-driven decision-making to monitor, influence, and control people in ways that weaken transparency, accountability, and individual rights. This chapter shifts focus from Venezuela to Xinjiang, highlighting how alleged human rights abuses in a major global power are different from those in a failing state, particularly through an advanced society with very advanced surveillance abilities. The Xinjiang case study does incorporate much of the previous information developed thus far. First, the study depicts how post–Cold War universalist language regarding atrocities and "never again" is applied or not applied and when the alleged perpetrator happens to be a major world and economic power. Second, it establishes a new role in digital surveillance and artificial intelligence in modern repression practice. Third, this study makes apparent how human-rights enforcement migrates into trade, sanctions, and corporate due-diligence regimes, evidenced by and through import bans tied to forced labor. Finally, this again provides another revealing context for Trump-era and post-Trump policies, which does combine anti-globalist discourse with an activist use of human-rights language and strategies against a well-known rival[28] The Xinjiang case study will again demonstrate how human rights enforcement can and does adapt when abuses are alleged in a technologically advanced globally integrated major power, highlighting the role of digital surveillance and artificial intelligence in modern repression.

Chapter Notes

[1] Human Rights Watch. (2024). World report 2024: Iran. Human Rights Watch.

[3] Center for Strategic and International Studies. (2019, September 3). Are sanctions working in Venezuela? CSIS.

[5] Human Rights Watch. (2024). World report 2024: Iran. Human Rights Watch.

[6] U.S. Department of State, 2020

[8] Human Rights Watch. (2024). World report 2024: Iran. Human Rights Watch.

[9] Georgetown Journal of International Affairs. (2025, May 14). Oil licenses and repression: The human rights impact of sanctions policy in Venezuela.

[11] U.S. Congress. (2019). Elie Wiesel Genocide and Atrocities Prevention Act of 2018 (Public Law 115–441).

[13] Geneva Centre for Human Rights Advancement and Global Dialogue, 2023

[15] Council on Foreign Relations, 2021

[17] Wall Street Journal, 2025

[19] Reuters. (2025, April 28). Trump's first 100 days: America First president is overturning world order. Reuters. (URL format will depend on final article slug; any copied

[21] Chatham House, 2022

[24] Atlantic Council, 2022

[26] Georgetown Journal of International Affairs. (2025, May 14). Oil licenses and repression: The human rights impact of sanctions policy in Venezuela.

[28] Roberts, 2020 (European Parliament, 2022 (Uyghur Human Rights Policy Act of 2020

Chapter 5: Xinjiang: Surveillance, Genocide Claims, and Algorithmic Authoritarianism

Over the past ten or so years the Xinjiang Uyghur Autonomous Region has been labeled one of the most heavily documented human-rights abuse situations in the world. UN assessments, NGO investigations, satellite imagery, and survivor testimony all converge and depict a large-scale arbitrary detention, pervasive surveillance, forced labor risks, and campaigns of cultural and religious assimilation targeting Uyghurs and other predominantly Muslim groups.[4] The UN Office of the High Commissioner for Human Rights has concluded that the extent of arbitrary and discriminatory detention, combined with broader rights restrictions, may amount to international crimes, in particular crimes against humanity.[3] China categorically has rejected these allegations of abuses. Officials announce policies in Xinjiang as being counterterrorism, deradicalization, and poverty alleviation, and emphasize economic development and security. Beijing's economic leverage and diplomacy have helped to deflect and fragment multilateral responses, and a significant number of states either support or remain neutral toward China's narrative in United Nations forum.[2] For this book's purposes, Xinjiang offers a different kind of measuring tool than Venezuela. It simply asks how the modern-day human-rights system reacts when confronted with a technologically sophisticated and globally integrated authoritarian state.[1]

Internment and criminalization

Beginning around 2017 to present, researchers have documented a vast network of "re-education" or "vocational training" facilities in Xinjiang, existing beside steep increases in criminal sentences and various forms of coercion. Details across NGO reports have described internment centers where detainees are restrained without meaningful due process, subjected to political indoctrination, and punished for ordinary religious or cultural expression.[7] These reports highlight patterns that include mass arbitrary detention, torture and ill-treatment, enforced disappearances, and persecution based on ethnicity and religion.[6] At the same time, official criminal statistics and court judgments indicate a sharp rise in prison sentences for vaguely defined "terrorism" or "extremism" offenses, effectively shifting some forms of detention from administrative to criminal channels while maintaining severe constraints on fair trial rights.[5]

Beyond the camps

Scholars have emphasized that the camp system is not a singled-out method of control. Internment is entrenched within a campaign-style governance that includes a considerable amount of neighborhood-level surveillance, intrusive home visitations, pressuring religious leaders, restrictions on language and cultural practice, and policies directly affecting birth rates and family structures.[10] Family separations are a recurring theme in testimonies: children are placed in state boarding schools or "orphanages" while parents are detained or pressured to participate in labor and "education" schemes.[9] In this sense, Xinjiang is not just a story of exceptional sites but of everyday life transformed under a mesh of legal, administrative, and technological control.[8]

Xinjiang has become an example case study of algorithmic authoritarianism: i.e. the use of big data, artificial intelligence, and networked technologies to identify, categorize, and manage populations. European Parliament analyses and independent researchers describe an "unprecedented surveillant assemblage" that combines biometric databases, facial and gait recognition, phone and app monitoring, and region-wide checkpoints.[15] Central to this system is the Integrated Joint Operations Platform, a data-fusion system that aggregates information on people's movements, communication patterns, electricity use, religious practices, and social ties. Individuals can be flagged as suspicious based on opaque criteria, including lawful behavior redefined as indicators of extremism.[14] Investigations have traced how Chinese and foreign companies supplied hardware, software, and services used for facial recognition, voice analysis, and other surveillance applications linked to Xinjiang. Some firms have since been sanctioned or added to export-control lists, while others have quietly exited or rebranded their operations.[13] Recent scholarship on internment governance suggests that digital tools and political ideology interact closely: algorithms help segment detainees, guide "risk assessments," and track supposed ideological transformation, while reducing transparency and human oversight.[12] Xinjiang thereby forces the human-rights field to grapple with transnational responsibility for digital tools: export controls on surveillance technologies, corporate due diligence in AI and biometrics, and the risk that techniques developed in one jurisdiction diffuse globally.[11] These are all very serious implications not only for the citizenry of China, but the technology being harnessed by other nation-states to essentially monitor and control them as well. This is just one of many problems with this human rights infringement. What about the right to privacy? Just a few months ago and 2 years ago I personally experienced government controls and surveillance as facial recognition is now being deployed in airports in travel situations. On departure from NY to Las Vegas, the airport used facial recognition as well as license/passport identification in a very interesting manner. Upon arrival in the Dominican Republic 2 years ago, the airport also utilized AI to screen facial recognition as well as our passports. How much more AI is really being used globally and for what reasons other than in the Peoples Republic of Xinjiang?

How should the patterns of abuses in Xinjiang be characterized from a legal perspective? Here, the case study reveals the politics of atrocity human rights law. The UN human-rights office has concluded that the documented arbitrary detention, discriminatory policies, and associated abuses may constitute international crimes, especially crimes against humanity, including imprisonment, persecution, and inhumane acts.[21] Major NGOs, drawing on interviews, satellite imagery, and leaked documents, similarly describe the situation as amounting to crimes against humanity directed against Turkic Muslim populations.[20] Several governments have gone further, formally determining that the Chinese government's actions in Xinjiang constitute genocide and crimes against humanity, citing evidence of coercive birth-prevention policies, forced sterilizations, and an intent to break the lineage and identity of Uyghurs as a group.[19] Parliaments or parliamentary bodies in other states have issued resolutions or statements using genocide language or strongly condemning atrocities, although these vary in legal framing and practical impact.[18] Legal scholars still remain divided. Some argue that the cumulative evidence satisfies multiple acts enumerated in the Genocide Convention, particularly relating to preventing births and forcibly transferring children. Others stress that the elements of crimes against humanity are clearer and warn about political consequences of genocide designations in the absence of adjudicatory forums.[17] For the purposes of this book, the key point is that the choice between "crimes against humanity" and "genocide" affects diplomatic pressure, sanctions narratives, and expectations of future accountability, especially given the absence of credible paths to an international criminal tribunal in the current geopolitical configuration.[16] What's being said by the scholars in this field is that their lacks mechanisms to legally change or to hold accountable this nation-state or its leadership for known horrendous human rights abuses. In this modern state of human rights, how can this be expected? The answers are unclear at this time.

UN mechanisms and political constraints

Within the UN system, Xinjiang has become a focus of treaty bodies, special rapporteurs, and the High Commissioner's office. These actors have raised concerns about mass detention, misuse of counter-terrorism frameworks, and restrictions on religion and culture, and have pressed for access and transparency.[25] Yet attempts to establish a full-fledged investigative mechanism with a mandate like those for Myanmar have so far failed, blocked or diluted by coalitions of states aligned with or influenced by China. Votes at the Human Rights Council have been closely contested, reflecting the intersection of economic ties, diplomatic alliances, and concerns about precedent.[24] Xinjiang thus illustrates both the sophistication and the vulnerability of post–Cold War human-rights machinery when it confronts a powerful state embedded in global governance structures.[22]

Sanctions and forced-labor legislation

Outside the UN, Xinjiang has is in the center of the thick array of sanctions and human-rights legislation, particularly in the United States and Europe. During Trump I, Congress adopted the Uyghur Human Rights Policy Act, directing the U.S. government to identify and sanction officials responsible for abuses in Xinjiang and requiring reports on surveillance, detention, and transnational harassment of Uyghurs.[30] Perhaps the most far-reaching step came with the Uyghur Forced Labor Prevention Act, which created a rebuttable presumption that goods linked to Xinjiang or certain entities are produced with forced labor and therefore barred from import. This effectively shifts the burden of proof onto companies and importers.[29]. Under subsequent administrations, enforcement has intensified: authorities have expanded the list of entities presumed to be involved in forced labor, issued guidance to companies on supply-chain tracing, and detained or blocked shipments of textiles, solar components, and other products.[28] The European Union, United Kingdom, Canada, and other actors have adopted targeted sanctions on officials and entities associated with Xinjiang and have moved toward broader regimes on supply-chain due diligence and import bans related to forced labor.[27] These are significant steps to perhaps slow-down a globalized powerful state as several nation-states have recognized the human rights atrocities and taken measures even if to not stop these behaviors, but maybe to deter in a financial way. However, will this actually change anything will remain to be seen.

Corporate presence and normalization

These profound abuse actions in Xinjiang have simply not been stopped. Reports by advocacy groups criticize multinational hotel chains and other firms for continuing to operate in the region, sometimes in partnership with state-linked entities, raising concerns that these investments normalize Xinjiang as a tourism and commercial destination while systemic abuses persist.[33] Here again we have multinationals partnering with abusive governments despite their atrocious human rights records. Investigations into technology and surveillance supply chains likewise suggest that foreign companies have provided components or services used in Xinjiang's security infrastructure, despite growing regulatory scrutiny.[32] Xinjiang continue to do business as usual. These developments highlight a wide shift in human-rights enforcement toward trade and corporate regulation, even as the underlying power asymmetries remain.[31]

The Xinjiang crisis extends beyond China's borders. Over the past decade, researchers and rights groups have documented patterns of transnational repression: pressure on other governments to repatriate Uyghur asylum seekers, intimidation of exiles' families, and surveillance of Uyghur communities abroad.[39] It appears that Chinas hand indeed is far reaching with significant influence as a major consumer[38]and seller of goods and services. Some nation states have cooperated with Chinese authorities by detaining or deporting Uyghurs, often in violation of the principle of non-refoulement, which prohibits returning individuals to places where they face a real risk of torture or other serious dangers.[37] Recent episodes of forced repatriation from third countries have triggered criticism by UN experts and Western governments, as well as targeted visa restrictions or other sanctions against officials involved in such transfers.[36] These cases raise difficult questions already hinted at in the Venezuelan context but sharpened here. What exactly are the obligations states have toward people fleeing a region where reputable bodies have alleged crimes against humanity or genocide, and how effectively can those obligations be enforced when strong economic and security incentives push in the opposite direction?[34]

Xinjiang provides an exemplary example in to trace the Trump-era discourse outlined earlier. During Trump I, the administration signed the Uyghur Human Rights Policy Act and backed sanctions on certain Chinese officials and entities linked to Xinjiang, even as it pursued a broader trade and geopolitical confrontation with China. Human-rights language about atrocities and camps mixed with discourse about economic competition and national security became paramount.[47] The administration that followed perpetuated and has deepened this discourse upholding the genocide determination, supporting multilateral statements at the Human Rights Council, and implementing the Uyghur Forced Labor Prevention Act as a central tool of rights-related trade policy.[44] Trump II did not dismantle this; instead, it has intensified their enforcement. The expansion of entity lists, stricter scrutiny of imports, and pressure on third countries not to repatriate Uyghurs indicate a willingness to use sanctions, visa restrictions, and trade measures aggressively in response to Xinjiang. (U.S. Customs and Border Protection (CBP), 2024[41] Simultaneously, the administration continues to criticize multilateral institutions and "globalist" constraints creating a familiar path, leveraging UN and NGO findings to justify unilateral action, while resisting multilateral oversight of U.S. conduct. This echoes the dynamic observed in

Venezuela but now applied to a much more powerful adversary.[40]

Xinjiang, like Venezuela, resists simple narratives of either triumph or the collapse of human rights. Instead, it highlights an ambiguous but multilayered reality. First, this case underscores the growing gap between documentation and enforcement. Previously the abuses have been in a remote region so extensively documented through UN reports, NGOs, academic research, and commercial satellites, yet this visibility has not translated into an effective multilateral enforcement mechanism. [57] Second, Xinjiang shows how human-rights enforcement is shifting toward economic and technological levers, targeted sanctions, forced-labor presumptions, export controls on surveillance technologies, and corporate due-diligence duties. These measures can have real impact, but they move key decisions into trade ministries, customs agencies, and corporate compliance teams, actors whose priorities may not fully align with victims' needs. [56],[54] Third, the case brings to light important questions about the globalization of surveillance and AI. The tools deployed in Xinjiang—biometrics, data fusion platforms, predictive policing are not unique to one jurisdiction; they are part of a wider contest over standards, exports, and norms that will shape human-rights protection and violation globally.[53] Fourth, Xinjiang exposes selective solidarity and geopolitical trade-offs. States that invoke universal human rights or religious solidarity in some contexts may remain muted here due to economic ties or strategic calculations, while states that condemn China are themselves criticized for their own practices on migration, policing, or counterterrorism.[52] Finally, Xinjiang reinforces a central thread in this book in that Trump I and Trump II do not mark a straightforward exit from human-rights politics. They operate squarely within human-rights discourse—adopting genocide language, expanding sanctions and forced-labor regimes, and pressuring third world states on refoulement while simultaneously challenging multilateralism and while asserting sovereignty in other domains.[50] Taken together with Venezuela, the Xinjiang case suggests that the "state of modern-day human rights" is best understood as a set of overlapping issues. In each, rights, institutions, and discourse are presented; yet positive or negative outcomes are again shaped by power, interdependence, and technology. The citizens most affected are detainees, separated families, and migrants, and they remain largely excluded from how and where strategies are designed, even as those strategies are justified in their names. The chapters that follow will examine in depth U.S. immigration detention to trace how these mechanisms and discourse operate under the different configurations of conflict, territory, and power. I will also be examining with detail some important terminologies associated with the middle east and human rights. Thus far we have learned more about who can, and cannot, realistically expect protection from the state of today's modern-day human-rights systems.

Chapter Notes

[1] Roberts, 2020 (European Parliament, 2022

[2] Office of the United Nations High Commissioner for Human Rights [OHCHR](Asia-Pacific Centre for the Responsibility to Protect, 2020 (Ryan, 2021

[3] OFFICE OF THE UNITED NATIONS HIGH COMMISSIONER FOR HUMAN RIGHTS [OHCHR], 2022A

[4] OFFICE OF THE UNITED NATIONS HIGH COMMISSIONER FOR HUMAN RIGHTS [OHCHR], 2022A (Human Rights Watch, 2021 (Amnesty International, 2021

[5] Greitens, Lee, & Yazici, 2020 (OFFICE OF THE UNITED NATIONS HIGH COMMISSIONER FOR HUMAN RIGHTS [OHCHR], 2022A

[6] Human Rights Watch, 2021 (Amnesty International, 2021

[7] Human Rights Watch, 2021 (Amnesty International, 2021

[8] Greitens, Lee, & Yazici, 2020

[9] OFFICE OF THE UNITED NATIONS HIGH COMMISSIONER FOR HUMAN RIGHTS [OHCHR], 2022A (Amnesty International, 2021

[10] Greitens, Lee, & Yazici, 2020 (Millward & Peterson, 2020

[11] European Parliament, 2022 (Qiang, 2021

[12] Millward & Peterson, 2020 (Qiang, 2021

[13] CENTER FOR STRATEGIC AND INTERNATIONAL STUDIES [CSIS], 2022 (U.S. Department of State, 2024 (Country Reports on Human Rights Practices: China (Murphy, Elimä, & Hallam, 2020

[14] OFFICE OF THE UNITED NATIONS HIGH COMMISSIONER FOR HUMAN RIGHTS [OHCHR], 2022A (Qiang, 2021

[15] European Parliament, 2022 (Qiang, 2021

[16] Lim, P. J. (2025). Combatting Uyghur forced labor: Trade law, supply chains, and human rights. Utah Law Review, 2025(2), 305–352.

[17] Lim, 2025 (Bacon, 2024

[18] Lim, P. J. (2025). Combatting Uyghur forced labor: Trade law, supply chains, and human rights. Utah Law Review, 2025(2), 305–352.

[19] U.S. Department of State, 2023 (Uyghur Forced Labor Prevention Act enforcement strategy / fact sheet (Uyghur Forced Labor Prevention Act of 2021 (Lim, 2025

[20] Human Rights Watch, 2021 (Amnesty International, 2021

[21] OFFICE OF THE UNITED NATIONS HIGH COMMISSIONER FOR HUMAN RIGHTS [OHCHR], 2022A

[22] Ryan, S. (2021). Atrocity crimes in Xinjiang: Moving beyond legal labels. Global Responsibility to Protect, 13(3), 215–244.

[24] OFFICE OF THE UNITED NATIONS HIGH COMMISSIONER FOR HUMAN RIGHTS [OHCHR], 2022B

[25] OFFICE OF THE UNITED NATIONS HIGH COMMISSIONER FOR HUMAN RIGHTS [OHCHR], 2022A (United Nations Special Procedures, 2025

[27] European Union, 2024 (UK Foreign, Commonwealth & Development Office, 2021

[28] U.S. Department of State, 2024 (Country Reports on Human Rights Practices: China (U.S. Customs and Border Protection [CBP], 2024

[29] Uyghur Forced Labor Prevention Act of 2021 (U.S. Customs and Border Protection [CBP], 2024, An effective piece of legislation

[30] Uyghur Human Rights Policy Act of 2020 (U.S. Department of State, 2024 (Country Reports on Human Rights Practices: China

[31] Ryan, S. (2021). Atrocity crimes in Xinjiang: Moving beyond legal labels. Global Responsibility to Protect, 13(3), 215–244.

[32] CENTER FOR STRATEGIC AND INTERNATIONAL STUDIES [CSIS], 2022 (Murphy, Elimä, & Hallam, 2020 (Qiang, 2021

[33] Murphy, Elimä, & Hallam, 2020

[34] Tobin, D. (2022). Genocidal processes and social death in Xinjiang. Ethnic and Racial Studies, 45(9), 1635–1657.

[36] U.S. Department of State. (2023). 2023 country reports on human rights practices: China (includes Hong Kong, Macau, and Tibet).

[37] United Nations experts, 2022 (Asia-Pacific Centre for the Responsibility to Protect, 2020

[38] European Parliamentary Research Service. (2023). An EU ban on products made using forced labour (PE 739.356). European Parliament.

[39] Tobin, 2022 (Uyghur Human Rights Project & Oxus Society, 2021

[40] Human Rights Watch. (2025, April 30). Venezuela: Brutal crackdown since elections. Human Rights Watch.

[41] U.S. Department of State. (2023). 2023 country reports on human rights practices: China (includes Hong Kong, Macau, and Tibet).

[44] U.S. Department of State. (2023). 2023 country reports on human rights practices: China (includes Hong Kong, Macau, and Tibet).

[47] Uyghur Human Rights Policy Act of 2020, Pub. L. No. 116-145, 134 Stat. 648 (2020).

[50] Uyghur Human Rights Policy Act of 2020, Pub. L. No. 116-145, 134 Stat. 648 (2020).

[52] Asia-Pacific Centre for the Responsibility to Protect. (2020). Genocide and crimes against humanity in Xinjiang? Applying the legal tests. University of Queensland.

[53] European Parliament, 2022 (Qiang, 2021

[54] Ryan, S. (2021). Atrocity crimes in Xinjiang: Moving beyond legal labels. Global Responsibility to Protect, 13(3), 215–244.

[56] European Union. (2024). Regulation (EU) 2024/3015 of the European Parliament and of the Council of 23 October 2024 on prohibiting products made with forced labour on the Union market. Official Journal of the European Union.

[57] Human Rights Watch, 2021 (Ryan, 2021

Chapter 6: Islamic Human Rights, Cultural Relativism, and the Middle East

In Chapter 3 I introduced cultural relativism in broad measures which included the idea that human-rights discourse can't necessarily be neutralized across civilizations, but are rather rooted in histories, cultures, and moral traditions. There I focused on the generic discourse and "Asian values" counter arguments. In this chapter I focus on a more specific and influential version of the relativist claim and Islamic human-rights concepts, and how they often frame Middle Eastern policies. The Middle East has amassed an extensive very long history. Often it has been singled out relentlessly for human-rights controversies, which include but are not exclusive to gender laws, blasphemy and apostasy, security practices, protest, and minority rights. It is also the region where numerous attempts to craft explicitly "Islamic" human-rights charters are developed, and where states and scholars have claimed that global human-rights law must be interpreted through an Islamic interpretation rather than a secular or liberal one.[3] My goal in this chapter is not to resolve or fully interpret theological or philosophical disputes. Instead, it is to show how this notion of cultural relativism is institutionalized in regional human-rights documents, and how those documents are invoked in practice when Middle Eastern governments face sustained criticism. I therefore choose to analyze both sides of the debate. First, the relativist "Islamic human rights" side, which insists that universalism must be grounded in sharia and local moral orders. Second, the universalist or critical side, which argues that cultural relativism is often functioning as a shield for power, and that certain rights claims, gender equality, freedom of religion, bodily integrity, cannot simply be relativized away.

The modern human-rights regime is typically traced back to the Universal Declaration of Human Rights (UDHR) in 1948 and the two binding covenants that followed on civil and political rights, and economic, social and cultural rights. These documents aspire to universality as they are considered as rights held "by all members of the human family" irrespective of culture, religion, or political system.[6] From inception, top representatives from both Arab and Muslim-majority countries helped to draft those standards. However, by the late 20th century, a handful of governments and scholars in the Middle East claimed the UDHR and its related treaties were indicative of a Western, secular land, and more liberal heritage that could not be adopted 100 percent within Islamic societies.[4] Meantime, in 1990, the Organization of the Islamic Conference (now Cooperation) adopted their own Cairo Declaration on Human Rights in Islam (CDHRI). This is an explicitly Islamic alternative doctrine compared with the western version the UDHR. The Cairo language is drafted in rights language and speaks of "dignity" and "freedom." But its structure distinguishes that rights and freedoms are repeatedly framed as gifts from God rather than being inherent as described in the UDHR.

Many articles end by stating that their implementation is "subject to the Islamic sharia."

Certain rights, in particular the fields of family law, religion, and public morality are spelled out in ways that diverge from international human-rights treaties.[12] However, in contrast, the Cairo Declaration affirms equality of human beings in dignity but allows for a differentiation in rights and duties between men and women within the family and it speaks of religious freedom but does not recognize a right to change one's religion (apostasy). It protects freedom of expression, but only insofar as expression does not violate principles of sharia.[10] In contrast with these, experts argue including United Nations officials, as well as independent scholars, that a built-in subordination to sharia law allows states wide discretion to override rights on religious grounds and undermines core protections in the UDHR and subsequent treaties.[8]

In 2020, the Organization of Islamic Cooperation adopted a revised declaration on human rights that replaced the 1990 Cairo text as its official rights doctrine. This new document moved closer in form to international human-rights language, incorporating many references to several UDHR-style rights, including some references to women's participation and to torture prohibition.[16] Significantly, the 2020 declaration no longer claims so consistently that all rights are subordinated to sharia in the same stylized way as the 1990 text. Many supporters have presented this as a sign that Islamic and international human-rights positions are converging, and as evidence that Muslim-majority states are willing to harmonize their positions with global standards.[14] This is a significant departure from the 1990 version, and it took 30 years for the middle east to begin to align with the western world in terms of what should be human rights with renewed respect for individuals outside of their religion. This alone represents a monumental change to what was thousands of year-old belief systems.

However, a lack of clarification still remains. Within the new declaration it still continues to reaffirm the heart of Islamic values and principles. Significant space is left for domestic law and "public morals" to limit human rights such as expression, assembly, and privacy. It does not clearly guarantee some of the most contested rights in international debates, such as full equality in family relations, freedom to change religion, or protection for sexual minorities.[20] From a universalist perspective, this new revision appears more like a mix of views and an improvement in rhetoric and language, but in no way a mirror of United Nations treaty standards. From an Islamic human-rights perspective, this new document can be read as an attempt to recast Islamic principles in a more globally legible idiom while maintaining a distinctive moral core.[17] This, in my opinion is still an enormous achievement for the middle east school of thought regarding strict adherence to sharia law and the evolvement to the 2020 declaration despite some specific reservations.

Advocates of cultural relativism in the Middle Eastern context present their case at several levels: theoretical, theological, and political. I have summarized the most common principles:

Human rights are not philosophically neutral

One strand emphasizes that the UDHR and its covenants arose from a particular historical compromise after World War II, rooted in European liberalism, Christian and secular thought, and the experience of specific atrocities. These instruments, proponents say, are not a timeless moral truth but one possible articulation of human dignity among others.[23] Saying this is to insist that every society adopt the UDHR principles without modification is itself a kind of cultural imperialism, and/or an attempt to export Western principles in the name of universalism.[21]

Divine sovereignty vs. popular sovereignty

Another significant contention is that this is within Islamic jurisprudence and political theology. In much of the modern human-rights discourse, sovereignty is explicitly grounded in "the people": governments derive their legitimacy from popular consent, and rights are constraints on state power on behalf of individuals.[27] Islamic human-rights scholars and those that consider this emphasize instead the sovereignty of God. Law, in this view, is not simply an instrument that citizens design; it must conform to divine revelation and the interpretive traditions built around it. Human beings possess dignity and rights, but those rights are understood within a framework where God's commands and prohibitions have normative priority.[26] Within this viewpoint, rights charters that contradict clear sharia rules on marriage, inheritance, modesty, or criminal penalties are seen as illegitimate attempts to override divine law with human preference. The Cairo and OIC declarations thus attempt to translate sharia-based moral commitments into the language of rights without abandoning their theological foundation.[25]

Social cohesion and moral order

Another contention is much more sociological. Some Middle Eastern intellectuals and officials argue that Western human-rights discourse emphasizes individual autonomy at the expense of community cohesion, family structures, and shared moral standards.[29] This viewpoint claims that unrestricted freedoms of expression, sexuality, and religious choice can destabilize societies, weaken family bonds, and erode the moral fabric. In this narrative, restrictions on pornography, blasphemy, public protest, or proselytism are portrayed not as violations but as necessary protections for social order and public morals.[28]

Critics of Islam and cultural relativism in the human-rights domain respond differently at multiple levels as would be expected.

Normative viewpoint

Universalists argue that certain rights such as freedom from torture and cruel punishment, equal dignity regardless of gender or religion, freedom of conscience and belief represent minimum conditions of human dignity cannot legitimately be overridden by culture or religion.[31] It is one thing to allow cultural variation in implementation (as an example, different institutional designs for social rights); it is another to permit practices such as stoning, flogging, imprisonment or execution for apostasy or blasphemy, or systematic discrimination against women in law, on the grounds of culture.[30] I agree that Donnelly's point is that these are not in alignment with what God would want anyway from a religious perspective…So how can this be justified in the name of God? Perhaps we are talking about more than one God? I do not wish to go to religious systems just trying to point out that the Sharia seems more like a means to subordinate than to justify with religious teachings.

Who is authority for "culture"?

Critics continue to ask: who gets to define "Islamic culture" or "Middle Eastern values"? In practice, charters like the Cairo Declaration were negotiated and signed by governments with poor rights records, often authoritarian regimes, not by broad-based democratic deliberation within Muslim societies.[40] Women's groups, minority organizations, and reformist religious scholars frequently challenge state-sponsored interpretations of sharia and culture. They argue that appeals to "tradition" often reflect the interests of male-dominated political and clerical elites, rather than an unfiltered expression of community values.[37] The argument is again a Western Vs. Eastern philosophical approach to rights, which are not reflective of one another philosophically or culturally. This group has suggested that this cultural relativism notion will represent less as a respectful recognition of pluralism, and more as a rhetorical weapon used by nation-states to deflect criticism, restrict internal dissent, and avoid obligations under treaties they have themselves signed.[33] This is a popular view for those opposed to a state's rights to be sovereign and create laws to govern itself. Of course, many scholars agree and disagree. What matters in this context is that critics recognize that by virtue of being a sovereign state you may or may not be subject to other nation-states belief systems in how to properly govern and protect your own society. This is frequently overlooked in the cultural relativism discourse by academics and idealist leaning positions.

Gaps with international treaty obligations

Many Middle Eastern states are parties to major human-rights treaties such as the International Covenant on Civil and Political Rights (ICCPR), the Convention on the Elimination of All Forms of Discrimination against Women (CEDAW), and the Convention against Torture. When these same states invoke the Cairo Declaration or "Islamic human rights" to resist criticism, UN treaty bodies and independent experts point out inconsistencies between their practices and their own treaty commitments. Specifically cited are reservations to CEDAW that subordinate equality provisions to sharia in family law. Criminalization of apostasy or blasphemy despite ICCPR protections for freedom of religion and expression. Use of corporal punishments or due-process light anti-terrorism laws all despite CAT and ICCPR standards.[43] This is concerning from a universalist perspective in that similar yet distinct charters like Cairo do function as routes to deflect, allowing governments to claim they adhere to human rights while they narrow their content domestically.[41] This is seen repeatedly throughout the countries cited for human rights abuses past, present, and likely in the future.

Seemingly, the relativism and or universalism debate sometimes may seem distant. In practice, however, they shape arguments in United Nations forums, domestic courts, and street politics throughout the Middle East. United Nations Human Rights Council, treaty bodies, the UN Human Rights Council, and Middle Eastern states have often criticized some resolutions, for example, the sexual orientation and gender identity, or on blasphemy laws—as imposing and Western values are incompatible with Islamic teachings.[48] Understandably in that Islamic culture is opposite on these matters 360 degrees. In responding to these treaty bodies, several governments have justified reservations or non-compliance with reference to sharia or national culture, citing the Cairo Declaration as a more appropriate standard for their societies. (Office of the United Nations High Commissioner for Human Rights, n.d.) On the opposite side, independent experts from the region including women's-rights advocates, dissident jurists, and Islamic reform thinkers frequently submit shadow reports that argue the opposite: universal rights can be grounded in Islamic values without reproducing current state practices.[45] Not sure how that could actually happen because state practices are tied directly to Islamic values in nearly all contexts.

Domestic reforms and backlash

Within Middle Eastern countries, human-rights reforms are often spoke about like contests over authenticity. Advocates for change argue that criminalizing domestic violence, restricting child marriage, or expanding women's political participation is consistent with both international norms and core Islamic principles of justice and mercy.[52] Opponents may portray such reforms as imports from the West that threaten religious identity and family structures.[50] In many cases, governments alternate between these positions and on one hand invoking Islamic tradition to justify restrictions at one moment and then invoking compliance with global human-rights standards in another, depending on their audience.[49] This flip flopping is seen within many nation-states top leadership positions shown by taking one position in the name of human rights within their own territory while evoking and staging human rights failures in other countries that do not mirror their own positions.

Popular protests

Recent protest movements in Iran, Lebanon, Iraq, Algeria, and elsewhere have shown that average citizens don't actually argue behind either side of the cultural relativism debate: Slogans like "Women, Life, Freedom" in Iran invoke universal sounding inspirations but are also articulated in local moral vocabularies. Protesters often demand both dignity and social justice terms that resonate with international rights discourse and with Islamic ethical language.[55]. This most certainly would suggest that a unique relationship between culture and rights is much more complex than the profound discourse between Western person centered versus Eastern communitarianism. Many human rights activists are actively hybridizing global human-rights language with local traditions to contest both authoritarian governments and external hegemony.[54]

The reason I've spent time delving into Islamic human-rights theory and cultural relativism is not to incapsulate the Middle East into a position of "difference," but it's to better understand the discourse which governments and movements have used when human-rights controversies have become salient issues. In Israel/Palestine, some regional actors point out their criticism of Israel in universal human-rights terms yet reject similar universalist scrutiny of their own practices at home and argue that "Western" rights agendas are used selectively. In Iran, authorities often characterize women's-rights and protest movements as Western-influenced or culturally alien, even as Iranian feminists and dissidents insist that their demands are rooted in BOTH universal rights and Islamic values.[64] For this book's overall thesis to provide accurate information regarding the state of modern-day human rights, the Middle Eastern cultural relativism debate must illustrate three crucial points: Universality is contested but not absent. Islamic human-rights discourse claims their own version of universalism; they are not simply rejecting rights discourse but reinterpreting it.[62] Many scholars, academics, and analysts would say this is not out of alignment with being a real finding. Alternative charters can both expand and restrict. They may open internal debates about justice and dignity in Islamic terms, but they can also serve as instruments for governments to insulate themselves from external scrutiny.[61] Again, more language to help a nation-state protect their sovereignty. Victims and activists are not bound by state narratives. Across the region, reformist scholars, women's movements, and protesters creatively combine global human-rights language with local moral resources, challenging both Western double standards and authoritarian uses of "culture."[57] Not sure I agree with these scholars indicating that there are Western double standards along with an authoritarian usage of culture. What might be more imaginative, is to say that Western standards do not coincide neatly with Eastern standards. Within subsequent chapters we will test these arguments within specific contexts, the debates traced so far will again emerge, but not as abstract theories, but as vocabulary made living through which human rights are claimed, denied, and renegotiated.

Chapter Notes

[3] Organization of the Islamic Conference, 1990

[4] Mayer, 2012

[6] Office of the United Nations High Commissioner for Human Rights. (1948). Universal Declaration of Human Rights. United Nations.

[8] Mayer, 2012

[10] Organization of the Islamic Conference, 1990

[12] Organization of the Islamic Conference, 1990

[14] Organization of Islamic Cooperation Independent Permanent Human Rights Commission. (2020). OIC declaration on human rights. Organization of Islamic Cooperation.

[16] Organization of Islamic Cooperation Independent Permanent Human Rights Commission. (2020). OIC declaration on human rights. Organization of Islamic Cooperation.

[17] An-Na'im, 1995

[20] Organization of Islamic Cooperation Independent Permanent Human Rights Commission. (2020). OIC declaration on human rights. Organization of Islamic Cooperation.

[21] Renteln, A. D. (1990). International human rights: Universalism versus relativism. Sage.

[23] Beitz, 2009

[25] Organization of the Islamic Conference, 1990

[26] Mayer, 2012

[27] Freeman, M. (2011). Human rights: An interdisciplinary approach (2nd ed.). Polity Press.

[28] Baderin, M. A. (2003). International human rights and Islamic law. Oxford University Press.

[29] Renteln, A. D. (1990). International human rights: Universalism versus relativism. Sage.

[30] Donnelly, J. (2013). Universal human rights in theory and practice (3rd ed.). Cornell University Press.

[31] Donnelly, J. (2013). Universal human rights in theory and practice (3rd ed.). Cornell University Press.

[33] Donnelly, 2013, 2

[37] Mahmood, S. (2005). Politics of piety: The Islamic revival and the feminist subject. Princeton University Press.

[40] Organization of the Islamic Conference, 1990

[41] Mayer, 2012

[43] Office of the United Nations High Commissioner for Human Rights, n.d. (Bennoune, 2018b

[45] An-Na'im, 1995

[48] Bennoune, K. (2018). Universality, cultural diversity and cultural rights (Report of the Special Rapporteur in the field of cultural rights, A/73/227). United Nations General Assembly.

[49] Bayat, A. (2013). Life as politics: How ordinary people change the Middle East (2nd ed.). Stanford University Press.

[50] Bennoune, K. (2018). Universality, cultural diversity and cultural rights (Report of the Special Rapporteur in the field of cultural rights, A/73/227). United Nations General Assembly.

[52] An-Na'im, 1995

[54] Musawah. (2009). Framework for action: For equality in the family. Musawah.

[55] Amnesty International, 2023

[57] Mahmood, S. (2005). Politics of piety: The Islamic revival and the feminist subject. Princeton University Press.

[61] Organization of the Islamic Conference, 1990 (Organization of Islamic Cooperation, 2020

[62] An-Na'im, 1995

[64] UN Special Rapporteur on the situation of human rights in the Islamic Republic of Iran, 2024

Chapter 7: Borders as a Human-Rights Test

In earlier chapters, I treated U.S. human-rights discourse more as discourse aimed away from the US: sanctions, atrocity prevention, and the way that Washington narrates abuses within other states. Meantime, the post-Cold War human-rights system was never meant to stop at borders. The right to seek asylum and the prohibition on refoulement which is the return of people to persecution or serious harm—are core elements of the contemporary human-rights structures.[1] Because of this significant doctrine there's a need to clearly outline these important provisions regarding asylum and refoulment, so we can better recognize the state of modern-day human rights and perhaps a better grasp of what these really mean. This chapter returns the discourse to the U.S. border itself. We are asking how recent immigration and asylum policies fit into the patterns already described in this book: the thickening of global human rights standards, the clashes between universalism and state sovereignty, and the way Trump I, Biden, and Trump II presidencies have treated human rights as both reference points and even as obstacles. I'll focus on four critical questions: How have U.S. border and asylum policies evolved from pre-Trump baselines through Trump I, the Biden administration, and Trump II? How do these policies compare with human-rights related standards, and specifically, concern about access to asylum, non-refoulement, and humane treatment while in detention? How do different human rights actors to include executive officials, courts, non-governmental organizations, (NGOs), and international bodies propose these policies in the human rights discourse? What more specifically do the evolving border policies tell us about the state of modern-day human rights? As in the case of Venezuela, the story is not simply a backslide or some type of progression. It has become sequential reconfiguration within common legal structure.

Modern human-rights law definitely emerged in the aftermath of World War II with explicit concern for refugees and displaced persons. The Universal Declaration of Human Rights[7] proclaimed a right to seek and enjoy asylum from persecution. Later, refugee treaties and practice consolidated the principle of non-refoulement: states should not send people back to territories where they face persecution, torture, or other serious harm.[6] These standards do not necessarily or effectively abolish a nation-states border. Instead, they impose minimum obligations on states when confronted with people who claim a need for protection. In practice, however, governments retain wide control over who can reach their territory, how they are processed upon arrival, and which legal label will become most appropriate. The U.S. is an excellent illustration of these principles: It has incorporated non-refoulement into domestic law and recognizes asylum, withholding of removal, and protection under the Convention against Torture.[4] It conducts intricate precise procedures such as credible-fear interviews, defensive and affirmative asylum processes, and immigration courts, while on paper, these supports affect to those obligations. At the same time, it has developed a menagerie of restrictive measures (travel bans, "safe third country" arrangements, expedited removal, public-health expulsions, app-based gatekeeping, and large-scale detention) that condition or restrict access to those protections.[3] The U.S border therefore has become an important and visible testing ground for the themes of this book: There is universal human rights language coexisting with sovereignty claims, institutionalization while coexisting with backlash, and significant ongoing human-rights rhetoric by opposing sides in policy disagreements. Do these propose a problem for the state of modern-day human rights or are they mere measures deemed appropriate by a powerful government to protect a sovereign nations security? The debate continues and so does the human rights rhetoric that defines these issues.

Before 2017, U.S. border policy combined somewhat of an aggressive enforcement posture with a formal commitment to asylum access. People who had reached U.S. soil (or ports of entry) and expressed fear of return to their home country were supposed to receive a credible-fear screening, and those who passed could pursue full asylum or related protections.[9].These policies were in line with UN treaties and UDHR language and protocols seemingly. However, critics of the pre-Trump border system claimed: There had been expedited removal procedures with limited reviews. The use of immigration detention, including family detention, were used as a deterrent. Very significant backlogs that had left people waiting for years in legal limbo.[8]

One important piece of the pre-Trump human rights legislation was the Deferred Action for Childhood Arrivals (DACA) program, announced by the Obama administration in 2012. DACA did not create a new immigration category and did not offer a path to permanent residence or citizenship. Instead, it used existing executive authority over prosecutorial discretion to designate a specific group of undocumented immigrants who came to the United States as children and met a series of conditions as low priority for deportation and eligible for a renewable two-year "deferred action" and work authorization.[16] Qualified applicants had to show that they arrived before age sixteen, had lived continuously in the United States since 2007, were present and lacked lawful status on 15 June 2012, were in school or had graduated or served in the military, and had no serious criminal record.[15] In U.S. terms, DACA was presented as an internal enforcement-priorities decision: the executive cannot remove everyone, so it announces that certain people that had arrived here as "Dreamers" would be temporarily protected if they come forward, registered, and passed background checks.[14] In human-rights terms, however, DACA quickly took on a broader meaning. It was widely understood as a partial recognition of a class of "members without status": people who had spent most of their lives in the United States, spoke English as their primary language, attended U.S. schools, formed families and careers there, yet remained deportable at any time. For supporters, DACA therefore aligned with human-rights ideas of social membership, non-discrimination, and family unity and the claim that people who have grown up inside a society and built their lives there should not be expelled to countries they barely know.[13] Was this indicative of being truly in line with human rights principals, or again another system designed to preserve a nations security and sovereignty? The program also became regarded and discussed to be where sovereignty-centered and human-rights centered narratives seemed to collide. Critics argued that DACA exceeded the proper bounds of executive discretion and encroached on Congress's exclusive power to set immigration rules and named it to be a breakdown of the rule of law and a signal that irregular entry could eventually be rewarded with quasi-legal status.[12] However, its supporters responded that the alternative was to treat long-term residents who arrived as children as permanently deportable, often to states they left as toddlers, despite their deep factual integration into U.S. society. In their view, DACA was a limited, reversible administrative measure that mitigated what human-rights advocates see as the harshest consequences of rigid status rules.[11] The broad interpretation of DACA again leads back to what human rights discourse was truly meant to be and how it is to be interpreted. Different administrations, different interpretations. Does this help clarify the state of modern-day human rights? Trump I's attempts to rescind DACA challenged in federal court and partially blocked by the Supreme Court made these fault lines explicit.[10] For many DACA recipients, the threat of termination translated directly into risks of family separation, loss of livelihood, and removal to countries where they faced violence or radical uncertainty, illustrating how questions of executive power are experienced as questions of basic security and dignity. For the purposes of this book, DACA is therefore not just an immigration policy detail. It is an example of how arguments about membership, childhood arrival, and long-term residence are increasingly discussed in human-rights language, and how those claims are contested by sovereignty-first positions that insist the state may treat even deeply rooted residents as removable "aliens" if they lack the appropriate paperwork.

Again, this is problematic for true human rights proponents as well as for state sovereignty ally's and human rights theorists, and those truly affected.

At the same time that the Obama administration created DACA, which modestly expanded refugee resettlement in the region, and also experimented with in-country processing. It is fair to describe the pre-2017 regime as a mixture or blend of human rights: heavily enforced, yet appearing on paper to be committed to the idea that unauthorized entrants could seek asylum regardless of mode of entry. This baseline matters greatly in the state of modern-day human rights because Trump I, Biden, and Trump II all claimed, and still claim, in different ways, to be restoring "order" to a system portrayed as being broken.

Trump's first term brought a marked shift in tone and in certain practices. The overall logic was familiar from earlier chapters: a sovereignty-first anti-globalist rhetoric, combined with selective usage of rights language when useful to further policy goals.

Travel bans and stratified mobility

Early 2017 saw a series of travel-ban executive orders targeting nationals of certain Muslim-majority and other states. After litigation and revisions, the Supreme Court upheld a narrowed version under the president's authority to suspend entry of noncitizens deemed detrimental to U.S. interest.[18] From a human-rights perspective, these bans represented several things: They created a hierarchy of mobility, where some nationalities were effectively excluded from normal travel and refugee resettlement channels. They sent a signal that security concerns justified broad nationality-based exclusions, even when individualized vetting might have been possible.[17] Again, how has the state of modern-day human rights evolved with these measures now in place? Human rights advocates argued that these bans eroded the very principle that protection should not depend on nationality stereotyping and contributed to in an atmosphere of suspicion. Understandably these positions are easily argued and debated and can be supported.

"Zero tolerance," family separation, and remain in Mexico

The highlight of Trump I's border strategies was a maze of deterrence-oriented policies: The "zero-tolerance" policy criminally prosecuted all unauthorized border crossers, resulting in large-scale family separation when adults were detained and children classified as unaccompanied.[23] The Migrant Protection Protocols (MPP, "Remain in Mexico") forced many asylum seekers to wait in Mexico for their U.S. immigration hearings, often in dangerous encampments with limited access to counsel.[22] Cooperative agreements with Central American states sought to shift asylum processing away from the U.S., asserting that these states could serve as "safe" alternatives despite their own protection deficits.[21] Human-rights bodies and NGOs documented kidnappings, assaults, and other abuses against people stranded in northern Mexico under MPP and related measures, arguing that this amounted to indirect refoulement and effective denial of the right to seek asylum.[19] These policies were arguably not perceived as human rights centric but were argued probably more likely from a financial point of view in that the US had been expending resources in a way that the migrant seekers host countries should have been more responsible for? Not exactly sure what exact reasoning behind these policies were but again we see an administration making decisions that on one hand appear to be furthering sovereignty and security, while ignoring numerous notions behind the standards of human rights already in place and frequently cited in other terms under other conditions.

Title 42: health law as border wall

In March 2020, the administration invoked Title 42, a public-health statute, to summarily expel most migrants at the border without providing asylum screening, citing COVID-19.[25] Public-health specialists and human-rights groups argued that: The measure lacked a solid epidemiological justification, particularly as other cross-border movements continued. Title 42 functioned in practice as a de facto asylum ban, allowing rapid expulsions with minimal process.[24]. By the time Trump left office, millions of expulsions had taken place under Title 42 authority. In the language of this book, Trump I translated a sovereignty-heavy, anti-globalist position into concrete border practices that sharply narrowed access to protection, even while officials insisted the U.S. still respected non-refoulement "in principle." Again, two arguments, first, Covid-19 was a real epidemic in which the medical field had never seen before. The numbers of deaths and the crippling effects on understaffed hospitals, nurses, and doctors within the US, and the uncertainty of how to contain this lethal epidemic left decision makers in a position where further measures to protect states sovereignty seemed like the most appropriate way to handle a situation of vast and uncertain consequences.

The Biden administration campaigned on restoring asylum and reversing some of Trump I's most controversial policies. The records that followed have again been a blend: there were some genuine changes, as well as new forms of restrictions that, in key respects, reconstituted Trump-era barriers using different tools and rhetoric.

Ending some Trump policies, maintenance of others

Upon taking office, Biden rescinded certain travel bans, ended family separation as an official policy, and moved to terminate MPP.[29] Proponents of idealist human rights theory were very enthused with these measures. However, Title 42 regarding the Covid 19 epidemic remained in use for more than two years under the new administration, despite earlier efforts to end it. Litigation and political pressure from some states led the government to defend the policy in court until the underlying COVID-19 public-health emergency formally expired on 11 May 2023.[27] This seemed like more of a contracted or legal measure or period of time that title 42 had to stay in place once implemented and the threat had actually been contained. Conversely, human rights advocates discourse again demonstrated a familiar pattern: human-rights concerns were acknowledged rhetorically but were subordinated to domestic political and security considerations.[26]

The "Circumvention of Lawful Pathways" rule and CBP One

As Title 42 ended, the administration introduced a new regulatory framework: the "Circumvention of Lawful Pathways" (CLP) rule, widely described as a new version of an asylum transit ban.[37] Key elements included: A rebuttable presumption of ineligibility for asylum for many people who traveled through another country and then crossed the U.S.–Mexico border without prior authorization. Exemptions tied to the use of "lawful pathways", notably humanitarian parole for certain nationalities and appointments obtained through the CBP One smartphone application.[36]

Narrow exceptions for people who could show inability to use the app, prior denial of asylum in a transit state, or extraordinary circumstances.[35] Simultaneously, the CBP One app became the primary gatekeeper for asylum seekers seeking to present at ports of entry. Individuals in northern Mexico were instructed to secure appointments via the app; without one, they risked falling under the CLP rule's ineligibility presumption.[34] NGOs and human rights groups quickly documented these serious access problems as limited language options and technical glitches. These were also barriers for people without smartphones, stable internet, or digital literacy. Furthermore, heightened vulnerability for those forced to wait months in dangerous Mexican border regions for scarce appointment slots.[33] Supporters argued the system brought "order" and predictability, channeling arrivals into a controlled queue and incentivizing formal pathways.[31] Critics described the CLP rule and CBP One as an asylum deterrence regime by administrative design, one that conditioned access to a fundamental protection on the successful use of a phone application and on the willingness and capacity of transit countries to provide safety.[30] In analytical terms, Biden partially reversed Trump's rhetoric while institutionalizing a technological system that continued restricted access to protection, albeit with more legal justifications and humanitarian discourse. I'm not sure how this measure became justified. As an analyst of human rights, it's totally arguable, as the NGOs already have, that this incentive appeared to be completely disastrous for human rights and for very obvious reasons already mentioned. Trump's return to office in 2025 has not simply reinstated Trump I policies. It has layered additional restrictions and infrastructure-heavy measures onto the system he has now inherited.

Ending CBP One asylum access and tightening the gate

One of the administration's early moves was to end the use of CBP One as a primary mechanism for asylum appointments at ports of entry, cancelling many pending slots and reorienting the app toward limited travel and cargo functions instead.[46] The Trump II administration acknowledged the obvious challenges with the CBP appointment system. However, this did not reopen unconstrained walk-up access to asylum. Instead, Trump II intensified use of expedited removal and narrowed eligibility criteria in ways that have further reduced the likelihood that people arriving without prior authorization can even reach a full asylum hearing.[45] What is happening under the Trump II administration we have witnessed is the shutdown of CBP One and a replacement with nationwide expansion policies of expedited removal, allowing CBP and ICE officers to summarily deport people encountered almost anywhere in U.S. territory if they entered between ports of entry and cannot prove two years of continuous presence, without an automatic hearing before an immigration judge.[44] At the same time, the administration is operating on top of the higher screening standards introduced under the Biden-era Circumvention of Lawful Pathways rule and subsequent "border security" regulations, which replaced the traditional "credible fear" test with more demanding "reasonable possibility" or "reasonable probability" thresholds and narrowed the opportunities for review of negative decisions.[43] The combined effect is that people who arrive without prior authorization are now more likely to be channeled into fast-track procedures where failing a brief fear interview can lead directly to removal, with little time to find counsel and no chance to present their case in an outright full adversarial asylum hearing.[39], etc.) Pro immigration reformists see this as positive for the US expanding upon sovereignty and nation-states ultimate authority with stricter regulation of who will migrate to the US and for those that have already immigrated but cannot prove that under federal laws that they have a legal right to remain. This administration has revamped the immigration system and border control in a manner never seen before.

Expanded travel bans and securitized mobility

In mid and late 2025, Trump II administration issued new travel-ban proclamations under INA § 212(f), restoring and extending restrictions on nationals of a longer list of countries and on individuals traveling on certain documents, including Palestinian Authority travel documents. These proclamations imposed full suspensions of entry (for immigrants and non-immigrants) on nationals of multiple states designated as "countries of identified concern." They added partial bans on visa categories such as tourism, student, and exchange visas for additional states. Additionally linked the measures to security, vetting, and "foreign policy objectives."[49]. This administration emphasizes continuity while Supreme Court case law is upholding earlier bans, presenting them as legitimate exercises of sovereign power.[48]. Critics, including refugee advocates and allies abroad, who have viewed the expanded bans as a de facto re-racialization and re-politicization of mobility, undermining the idea that access to protection and family unity should not hinge on broad nationality judgments.[47]. The current administration appears to currently portray human rights policy as placing significant priority upon the state of modern-day human rights from a nation's sovereignty being first and foremost. Meantime nation-state security enforcement measures vs. human rights discourse compliance with already in-place human rights standards dating back to post-world war and post-cold war global standards are simply minimized or overlooked. These are simply being minimized to the point that our own allies are curious what our true agendas really are aimed at.

Warehouse detention and logistics-style deportation

Perhaps the most striking Trump II development is a plan outlined in draft procurement documents to convert industrial warehouses into large-scale immigration detention hubs with capacity for more than 80,000 people at any given time.[54] The proposal envisions seven regional "mega-warehouses," each holding 5,000–10,000 detainees near transportation and logistics hubs. Additionally, there will be mid-sized warehouse facilities accommodating up to 1,500 people each. Finally, intake sites that funnel newly arrested migrants into these hubs for rapid processing and deportation.[53] Officials frame the system as an efficiency measure, likening it to a modern logistics chain designed to move people through quickly, reduce costs, and standardize conditions.[52]. Again, as I mentioned earlier prior to this citation, reducing associated costs and standardizing conditions seem more of a priority than actually keeping a mindset that these may actually be truthful immigrants with legitimate reasons to flee their countries. Human-rights and immigrant-rights organizations respond that warehouses designed for storage are poorly suited to long-term habitation, raising serious concerns about health, ventilation, and humane treatment. Concentrating thousands of detainees in remote industrial zones impedes access to legal counsel, families, and independent oversight. The plan reflects a broader trend toward treating migrants less as rights-bearing individuals than as flows to be managed at scale.[51] In terms of this book, this warehouse plan is an example of institutional creativity applied to enforcement, with human-rights safeguards playing a reactive, and more secondary role.

Across these administrations, Trump I, Biden, Trump II—the border remains completely saturated with human-rights discourse. The situation, seemingly, is concerned with which rights, for whom, and under what conditions? More questions than answers seem to be foremost.

Protection of whom?

Governments justify restrictive measures, Title 42, transit bans, detention expansion, as necessary to: Protect public health, national security, or the integrity of the asylum system.[57];[56]. They additionally prevent deaths in transit by discouraging irregular journeys in dangerous conditions.

Preserve political support for any form of protection by demonstrating "control."

Advocates and humanitarian organizations counter that: Restrictive measures rarely end displacement; they redirect flows into more dangerous routes and leave asylum seekers exposed to kidnapping, exploitation, and violence in transit countries.[60] "Inhumane migration policies endanger lives at the US-Mexico border"[59]. Policies like the CLP rule, CBP One gatekeeping, expanded travel bans, and warehouse detention impose severe costs on economic, social, and family rights, often without delivering durable "order."[58]. Both sides of the debate increasingly use language of protection of either state and citizen security, or of vulnerable migrants which in turn relates to earlier chapters where human rights became a shared vocabulary for very different agendas. Unfortunately, these are how governments react to proposed threats to sovereignty, and security, as well as a perception of lessening their own citizens human rights while assuming and overmanaging needs of immigrating persons as being less important than their own citizens human rights and needs. Again, the principal assertion remains, a nation-state must protect its citizenry from questionable foreseeable problems and present working solutions.

Universality, sovereignty, and externalization

The evolving border dramatizes the clash between universalist and sovereigntist narratives: Universalist arguments emphasize the right to seek asylum upon arrival at a state's frontier and the absolute nature of torture and refoulement prohibitions.[64] Sovereigntist arguments stress a state's right to decide who enters, under what conditions, and to limit "abuse" of asylum through deterrence and procedural filters.[63]

Human rights related policies such as transit bans, "safe third country" transfers, and forced waiting in Mexico or elsewhere, represent a strategy of externalization as a shifting responsibility for protection onto other states or onto territories beyond the perimeter of robust legal oversight.[68] This argument will continue and is consistent with the way the current administration is being perceived by human rights advocates as well as the literal human rights language supporters. In the tremendous amounts of Trump-era rhetoric regarding human rights, externalization is being paired with skepticism toward international monitoring: United Nations bodies and non-governmental organizations (NGOs) are portrayed as being out of touch elites and idealists that are willing to interfere with democratic border controls, and meantime their reports also cite and condemn abuses by other governments.

Asymmetries of voice and visibility

As with Venezuela, those most affected by border and detention policies, the migrants, asylum seekers, and deportees, have limited direct influence over this design. Their experiences enter the records primarily through litigation and court testimony, and NGO and press reports documenting conditions and abuses. There are also occasional international inquiries or special rapporteur visits.[71];[70]. Yet the decisions themselves about Title 42, CLP, travel bans, warehouse contracts are all made in Washington, federal courts, and executive agencies balancing political pressures, security narratives, and institutional interests. This is an enormous part of the contemporary state of modern-day human-rights conditions with global standards to formally acknowledge migrants as rights-bearing subjects, but unfortunately institutionalized channels for them to shape the rules are increasingly narrow.

Seen alongside the previous chapters, the evolution of U.S. immigration and asylum policy underscores several diverse conclusions and interpretations. Firstly, human-rights commitments can be reshaped significantly. The U.S. has not withdrawn from the Refugee Convention policy. Instead, executives of different parties have developed public-health expulsions, transit bans, phone-application based gatekeeping, and massive detention centers that change when and how obligations are triggered, often with limited legislative input.[77]As signatories of refugee convention policies, the current administration appears to be to support these initiatives, but executives of both parties have reshaped the mechanisms they had initially agreed to regarding human rights mechanisms. Second, statutory and institutional creations have an extensive lasting impact. Tools introduced under one administration (expedited removal, Title 42 processes, asylum-limiting regulations) can be maintained, modified, or repurposed by successors, just as atrocity-prevention and sanctions tools can survive the officials who first invoked them.[75] Third, the border has become a central stage for anti-globalist politics. Trump-era actors portray international refugee discourse, UN criticism, and NGO reports as elite or foreign intrusions into sovereign border control, while using selected international findings to justify hardline stances against other states and against migrants themselves.[72]This rhetoric is likely to continue especially along party lines given the history of past and current administration's policies and priorities. Fourth, the case illustrates the elusiveness of human-rights and security policy. Immigrant detention warehouses, travel bans, and phone application mediated access to ports of entry are justified in terms of security, order, and capacity, yet they have direct and unprecedented hardship effects on the enjoyment of human rights by a very large very vulnerable population. Finally, and most importantly for this book, the border shows how universality remains deeply conditional. In principle, any persons fleeing persecution should be able to claim asylum. In practice, their chances depend on nationality, timing, access to technology, geography, and the shifting priorities of administrations committed to very different visions of sovereignty, globalism, and security. Again, the mechanisms to deal with this are in place, but their enforcement remains uncertain at best. The border story should still remain in mind as it reveals how a major power can operate in the human-rights discourse and continuously determine just how far it can stretch the distance between formal commitments and actual pro human rights support.

Chapter Notes

[1] UNHCR, 2025 (United Nations, 1951

[3] American Immigration Council. (2022, April 29). A guide to Title 42 expulsions at the border. American Immigration Council.

[4] American Immigration Council, 2023

[6] UNHCR, 2025

[7] 1948

[8] Bersin, Bruggeman, & Rohrbaugh, 2024

[9] American Immigration Council, 2023

[10] Department of Homeland Security v. Regents of the University of California, 591 U.S. ___ (2020).

[11] Sirriyeh, A. (2020). 'Dreamers', (un)deserving immigrants and generational interdependence. Population, Space and Place, 26(8), e2370.

[12] Meissner & Gelatt, 2020

[13] Cortes Romero, L. (2020, April 27). Activism leads, the law follows: DACA and its fate at the Supreme Court. Human Rights Magazine, American Bar Association.

[14] Congressional Research Service. (2021, April 14). Deferred Action for Childhood Arrivals (DACA). Congress.gov

[15] U.S. Citizenship and Immigration Services. (2025, January 24). Consideration of Deferred Action for Childhood Arrivals (DACA).

[16] Department of Homeland Security. (2012, June 15). Exercising prosecutorial discretion with respect to individuals who came to the United States as children.

[17] Lutheran Immigration and Refugee Service. (2017, January 25). Lutheran Immigration and Refugee Service condemns the Trump administration's actions against refugees and migrants. Refugee Council USA.

[18] Trump v. Hawaii, 585 U.S. ___ (2018).

[19] Human Rights First. (2025, January 10). Remain in Mexico: Unlawful, ineffective, and must never be repeated. Human Rights First.

[21] McDonnell, T. M. (2025). Unsafe at any speed: "Safe Third Country Agreements"—Offshoring and eroding legal protections owed to refugees and asylum seekers. Fordham Urban Law Journal, 53(1), 17.

[22] American Immigration Council. (2024, February 1). The "Migrant Protection Protocols": An explanation of the Remain in Mexico program. American Immigration Council.

[23] U.S. Department of Justice Office of the Inspector General, 2021

[24] American Immigration Council. (2022, April 29). A guide to Title 42 expulsions at the border. American Immigration Council.

[25] American Immigration Council. (2022, April 29). A guide to Title 42 expulsions at the border. American Immigration Council.

[26] Edlow & Ries, 2022

[27] American Immigration Council. (2022, April 29). A guide to Title 42 expulsions at the border. American Immigration Council.

[29] The White House, 2021 (U.S. Department of Homeland Security, 2021

[30] National Immigration Project of the National Lawyers Guild, 2023 (Electronic Privacy Information Center, 2023

[31] Department of Homeland Security. (2023, May 11). Fact sheet: Circumvention of lawful pathways final rule.

[33] American Immigration Council, 2023 (International Rescue Committee, 2024

[34] American Immigration Council, 2023

[35] Murray Osorio PLLC. (2024, November 1). Understanding the Biden Administration's Circumvention of Lawful Pathways Rule (CLP).

[36] Congressional Research Service, 2024 (National Immigration Project of the National Lawyers Guild, 2023

[37] Congressional Research Service, 2024

[39] National Immigration Forum, 2025

[43] Congressional Research Service, 2024

[44] National Immigration Forum, 2025 (National Immigration Law Center, 2025 (Migration Policy Institute, 2025

[45] American Immigration Council, 2023 (Congressional Research Service, 2024

[46] Texas Standard. (2025, January 24). Trump stopped usage of the CBP One app at the border. Here's what that means.

[47] Global Refuge. (2025, December 16). Global Refuge deeply alarmed by expansion of sweeping travel ban.

[48] The White House, 2025

[49] The White House, 2025 (NAFSA, 2025

[51] The Washington Post, 2025

[52] The Washington Post, 2025

[53] The Washington Post, 2025.

[54] The Washington Post, 2025

[56] Department of Homeland Security. (2023, May 11). Fact sheet: Circumvention of lawful pathways final rule.

[57] American Immigration Council. (2022, April 29). A guide to Title 42 expulsions at the border. American Immigration Council.

[58] National Immigration Project of the National Lawyers Guild, 2023 (American Immigration Council, 2023 (The Washington Post, 2025

[59] MSF, January 13, 2023

[60] International Rescue Committee. (2024, November 1). What do President Biden's border policies mean for asylum seekers? International Rescue Committee.

[63] Congressional Research Service, 2024

[64] UNHCR, 2025

[68] National Immigration Project of the National Lawyers Guild. (2023, May 26). Biden's asylum ban: Practice advisory.

[70] American Immigration Council, 2023

[71] American Immigration Council. (2022, April 29). A guide to Title 42 expulsions at the border. American Immigration Council.

[72] Global Refuge. (2025, December 16). Global Refuge deeply alarmed by expansion of sweeping travel ban.

[75] Congressional Research Service, 2024

[77] American Immigration Council. (2022, April 29). A guide to Title 42 expulsions at the border. American Immigration Council.

Chapter 8: Human Rights in a Transactional World: What has changed in 2025, and Why

As I close this book, I want to briefly summarize the first 7 chapters and then analyze specifically human rights in 2025, the opening year of President Trump's second administration. In my first 7 chapters I've tried to be clear consistently; human rights are not just "good words" or "ideas". These are real protections that either exist in practice or they do not. I've begun to trace how the state of modern-day human-rights systems have grown after World War II, how the United States has helped shape portions of these, and how those standards have become a distinct moral discourse frequently cited in diplomacy, war, trade, and international pressure. I've also shown how, over time, human rights became something governments have used although selectively, to promote them when convenient and downplay them when inconvenient. Throughout the earlier chapters, I've focused on several consistent patterns: First, human rights often increase in relevance when the United States would like to present as a global example or when it's necessary to pressure a rival. But human rights concern often becomes less salient when other policy interests become a higher priority: national security, border control, counterterrorism, economic deals, energy prices, or strategic alliances. Second, I highlighted the gap between rhetoric and specific outcomes. Politicians of all parties talk about freedom and dignity, but people living under repression, in war zones, or in desperate poverty do not experience "human rights" as mere words. They have real and very negative experiences such as poor safety, no food, shelter, or legal protection, and the inability to live life without fear from repression. Third, I showed how migration and asylum have become one of the most important human-rights battlegrounds in the modern era. When people are transmigrating for various reasons to include violence, poverty, climate stress, or significant political repression, governments face scrutiny if they do not act. And far too often, a response is to push responsibility away from the border and relocate this responsibility into another country, with few protections and less accountability. Finally, I examined how courts, international bodies, and treaties have struggled to keep up with modern human rights realities. Even when measurable, internationally recognized laws exist, enforcement is often inconsistent. Powerful states have bent the rules, ignored them, or applied them unevenly. This is one reason people around the world have grown cynical about the human-rights "system" and the rhetoric. They have noticed when rules are applied differently depending on who is considered. That brings us to 2025. The opening year of Trump's second term did not appear to be a brand-new era but much like a stronger version of events that were already underway. The world was already facing a major threat of war, major displacements, major economic pressures, and a growing anxiety in which global rules seem more optional.

Under these conditions, U.S. human-rights policy in 2025 is best understood in more simplified terms in that it has become more "hands-on" and more practical, but also more transactional. In other words, human rights have not disappeared from the human rights discussions, but, unfortunately, they frequently competed with other nation state priorities and more often frequently lost. To explain what this looked like realistically, it helps to segment 2025 into a handful of relevant policy areas and then analyze the countries that drew the most attention.

Sanctions, money, and oil

One of the significant places where human rights and hard political interests collide is sanctions. Sanctions are not just singled out as morality issues; they are about political pressure. And in 2025, Iran remained a very strong example of how human-rights discourse is often filtered through financial tools. With Iran, the Trump administration pushed a tough approach that aimed to threaten Iran's revenue, specifically through oil-related networks such as shipping, middlemen, and financial channels that keep significant amounts of money on the move. Supporters have argued and justified this by indicating Iran's government represses its people, funds proxy groups, and detains opponents and foreign nationals, and that pressure is justified. Of course, critics have argued that this type of broad pressure will hurt ordinary citizenry and does not always produce measurable human rights outcomes. But a key point for this book is simple: this particular policy was designed to restrict revenues as well as to increase leverage. It was not intended to be built around clear human-rights milestones that could be measured and then verified. That matters a lot, because when a policy is judged mainly by whether it disrupts oil income or changes behavior in a negotiation, human rights become more of a supporting reason than the main goal of the efforts. At the same time, 2025 also showed something that is easily missed if we only look at the discourse. There can be tough posturing without advancing into a war (with its own very significant challenges). During this timeframe, the U.S. could increase pressure through money and enforcement while still trying to avoid a wider military escalation. That combination can look inconsistent on the surface, but it could also be interpreted as a well-rehearsed strategy, apply pressure, keep all options available, and avoid escalation into a war unless and only unless absolutely necessary. On the other hand, Saudi Arabia does not mirror this particular example. If Iran demonstrates coercion, Saudi Arabia shows more of a partnership. In 2025, the U.S.–Saudi relationship continued to show that human rights often became secondary when energy markets and regional security are threatened or at stake. Public defenses of Saudi leadership had sent clear messages that the relationship would not be mainly judged by accountability for human rights abuses. This does not mean U.S. leadership had never mentioned human rights issues. In simpler terms, human rights do not consistently control this relationship the way other interests do. For my diverse readership, liberal, conservative, Republican, Democrat, this is the uncomfortable reality, when oil prices matter, when security cooperation matters, and when regional influence matters, human-rights pressure tend to be less politicized. There becomes less of a consistent amount of negative discourse and more symbolic talks and negotiations.

War, peace deals, and civilian suffering

If sanctions are one arena where rights collide with interests, war is whole other, and in 2025, Gaza and Ukraine had dominated global attention. In Gaza, the Trump administration's role had supported ceasefire efforts, plans for what to do next, and to push for stabilization. The human-rights problems here are not too difficult to understand, stopping the killing is urgent, but stopping the killing is not equal to real justice. Ceasefires can save lives short-term. They can also put into place a new "normalization" where deep human rights issues are never fully addressed. Human-rights groups have warned that humanitarian pauses, and reconstruction planning do not automatically or instantly bring or force accountability for civilian harm, fair treatment of detainees, or real protection for at risk civilians overall. The approach in 2025 seemed to portray human rights as something that could improve but only after the return of stability. This seems almost like better human rights are the reward for stability and order. The obvious risk here is that this could create a world where civilians are protected when powerful government actors decide it is useful, rather than because rules should be enforced. Ukraine and Russia looked different. In 2025, the U.S. pursued visible diplomacy while exploring possible answers and negotiations. Meantime, keeping major sanctions tools in place. Here, the conflict remained strongly tied to ideas of sovereignty, territorial integrity, and the laws of war. In comparison to Gaza, the human-rights discourse and international-law discourse remained more direct: who was the invader, who controls territory, and what happens to civilians under occupation or during attacks.

What does this tell us?

It tells us that the strength of human-rights language most often depends on the context. When U.S. alliances and international-law arguments coincide, the rights discourse remains firm. When alliances and politics are complicated, or when stability becomes the primary goal, human rights issues can be placed into a less talked- about position.

Migration and asylum: moving responsibility away from the border

Another major human-rights battleground in 2025 was migration and asylum. In plain terms, the big move in modern migration policy is to shift responsibility away from the United States—either to other countries or to systems that make it harder for people to reach a place where they can claim protection. In 2025, enforcement expanded and the government explored arrangements that would send some migrants to other countries rather than allowing them to remain in the U.S. during their process. Central American countries remained central to this concept, El Salvador, Honduras, Guatemala, because they are part of the migration route and a broad deterrence system. From a pro human-rights viewpoint, the biggest issues are not whether a country has borders. All countries do. The biggest importance becomes whether people who may be fleeing real verifiable dangers will be able to ultimately receive fair processing. This means access to asylum screening, access to legal help, and protections against being sent back into danger are in real danger. When responsibility is reverted to other countries with weaker processing systems and fewer safeguards, real accountability seems much more difficult. More powerful governments could say, "We handled it," even when the person's human rights remain completely unprotected. Inside the U.S., courts do sometimes limit certain enforcement measures. This can matter significantly. It demonstrates that rule-of-law constraint does still exist domestically. But those protections do not automatically follow people once they are outside U.S. borders or transferred into other systems. That alone creates an enormous problem between human rights and the real realities of enforcement of them.

Rule of law: international rules as tools, not limits

Across all these areas in 2025, one pattern emerged at the top: international laws were treated more like a tool than limitations. This does not look like tearing up human rights treaties or walking away from international institutions. Often this appears calm and practical more simplified, use international rules when they can help, and downplay them when they become less useful. This kind of selective approach is not unique to this Trump administration, and it is not limited to the United States. But when a powerful nation-state can ignore established rules as being optional, it sends a message to their allies and the rest of the world. Other states can then follow the same logic and processes. Over time, this can weaken human rights mechanisms not only because people ignore them, but because ignoring them becomes a natural way to conduct international relations.

Is this a flip-flop, or a consistent model?

Many critics describe 2025 as a year of reversals. But if we look at the larger picture, it could also be understood as a consistent model, more of a transactional human-rights policy method. In this model, human rights are still part of the discourse of powerful governments. They are not entirely erased. But they are frequently used as a supporting role and often lose out when competing priorities remain higher priorities. In summary, Iran: pressure through money and enforcement, without clear human-rights benchmarks. Saudi Arabia: partnership "alliances" continue, human-rights accountability is not treated as conditional. Gaza: heavy focus on ceasefires and stabilization, accountability less central.

Ukraine: diplomacy continues while sanctions and legalized discourse remain strong. Central America and migration: responsibility strongly shifted with a diversified approach diverting responsibility and then reducing direct accountability. This does not appear to be random. It suggests more of a hierarchy of priorities. Human rights remain in the discourse, but they are not consistently used in the main prioritized and organized principle. What this implies for the human-rights system worldwide:

The consequences of this policy go beyond any single nation-state

First, it speeds up the shift from universal human-rights discourse into more of a transactional human-rights discourse. Over and over, countries begin to treat human rights like bargaining measures: how much will this cost, what may we gain, what could we lose, who is critical of whom, and why is this happening? Second, this posturing places results over process. Governments emphasize reduced harm and restoration of order, sometimes for good reason, but unfortunately this could frequently cause significant delays to due process, accountability, and institutional reforms. In human-rights discourse, this could mean less guarantees and few lasting protection policy standards. Third, there is perceived to be an increase of dual standards. Allies receive flexibility; adversaries receive punishments. This selectivity makes it more difficult for human-rights language to persuade effectively. Citizens and critics can easily view and feel when the human rights rules do not feel equal.

Conclusion: America's future role under newer administrations and the current administration

The policies of 2025 do not represent a reversal of human rights priority but more of a culmination of events that began earlier in this decade. Whether under Trump or future administrations, the United States appears increasingly likely to approach human rights as one important variable among several, rather than as a singled out governing priority. This does not necessarily imply an inevitable decline of human-rights advocates or advocacy. It suggests more of a significant transformation. Future administrations will likely inherit responsibilities in which:

- Economic interests dominate human rights enforcement.
- Conflict diplomacy will prioritize stability over justice.
- Migration governance becomes more externalized.
- International law is selectively lessened and invoked accordingly. The challenges for modern human-rights advocacy, therefore, is not to restore the near invisible consensus, but to become effective within this transactional reality, this could be through developing metrics, coalitions, and accountability mechanisms acceptable to powerful nation-states that could survive in an era where moral authority alone can no longer drive human rights policy. If human rights are to remain relevant in U.S. foreign policy, they must be integrated but not as pure idealism, but as measurable constraints with measurable consequences. Whether newer administrations or the current administration chooses to make that integration will determine not only America's moral standing globally, but the future and credibility of the global human-rights discourse itself.

References

Al Jazeera. (2023, June 13). How are US sanctions affecting life in Venezuela? Al Jazeera.

www.aljazeera.com (link)

Al Jazeera. (2023, June 27). ICC to continue investigation of human rights abuses in Venezuela. Al Jazeera.

www.aljazeera.com (link)

AllSides. (2025, December 24). ICE plans to detain migrants in converted warehouses. AllSides. www.allsides.com (link)

American Immigration Council. (2022, April 29). A guide to Title 42 expulsions at the border. American Immigration Council. www.americanimmigrationcouncil.org (link)

American Immigration Council. (2024, February 1). The "Migrant Protection Protocols": An explanation of the Remain in Mexico program. American Immigration Council. www.americanimmigrationcouncil.org (link)

Amnesty International. (2005). USA: Guantánamo and beyond: The continuing pursuit of unchecked executive power (AMR 51/063/2005). Amnesty International. www.amnesty.org (link)

Amnesty International. (2018). Amnesty International report 2017/18: The state of the world's human rights. Amnesty International. www.amnesty.org (link)

Amnesty International. (2020). Amnesty International report 2019/20: The state of the world's human rights. Amnesty International. www.amnesty.org (link)

Amnesty International. (2021). "Like we were enemies in a war": China's mass internment, torture and persecution of Muslims in Xinjiang. Amnesty International.

[www.amnesty.org (link)](www.amnesty.org)

Amnesty International. (2024, December 10). Iran: New compulsory veiling law intensifies oppression of women and girls. Amnesty International.

[www.amnesty.org (link)](www.amnesty.org) Amnesty International

Amnesty International. (2024, May 8). USA: CBP One: A blessing or a trap? Amnesty International. [www.amnesty.org (link)](www.amnesty.org)

Amnesty International. (2025a). The state of the world's human rights. Amnesty International. [www.amnesty.org (link)](www.amnesty.org)

Amnesty International. (2025b). Chaos & cruelty: 10 compounding assaults on human rights: A review of President Trump's first 100 days in office. Amnesty International. [www.amnesty.org (link)](www.amnesty.org)

An-Na'im, A. A. (1992). Human rights in cross-cultural perspectives: A quest for consensus. University of Pennsylvania Press.

[books.google.com (link)](books.google.com)

Asia-Pacific Centre for the Responsibility to Protect. (2020). Genocide and crimes against humanity in Xinjiang? Applying the legal tests. University of Queensland.

[r2pasiapacific.org (link)](r2pasiapacific.org)

Atlantic Council. (2025, January 23). Maximum pressure sanctions on Venezuela help U.S. adversaries, hurt Venezuelans. Atlantic Council.

www.atlanticcouncil.org (link)

Bacon, E. (2024). Trade, human rights, and the Xinjiang crisis: Rethinking economic statecraft. Georgetown Journal of International Law, 55(1), 101–143.

scholar.google.com (link)"Xinjiang+crisis\"+trade+human+rights

Baderin, M. A. (2003). International human rights and Islamic law. Oxford University Press.

global.oup.com (link) Oxford University Press

Bayat, A. (2013). Life as politics: How ordinary people change the Middle East (2nd ed.). Stanford University Press.

doi.org (link)

Bell, D. A. (1996). The East Asian challenge for human rights. Human Rights Quarterly, 18(3), 641–667. doi.org (link)

Bennoune, K. (2018). Universality, cultural diversity and cultural rights (Report of the Special Rapporteur in the field of cultural rights, A/73/227). United Nations General Assembly.

www.ohchr.org (link)

Bersin, A. D., Bruggeman, N., & Rohrbaugh, B. (2024). Migration at the U.S.-Mexico border: A challenge decades in the making. Migration Policy Institute.
www.migrationpolicy.org (link)

Center for Strategic and International Studies. (2019, September 3). Are sanctions working in Venezuela? CSIS.

www.csis.org (link)

Center for Strategic and International Studies. (2022). Securing global supply chains: The Xinjiang challenge [Report]. CSIS.

www.csis.org (link)

Center for Strategic and International Studies. (2023, November 29). On the uses and misuses of Venezuela sanctions. CSIS.

www.csis.org (link)

Chishti, M., & Bush-Joseph, R. (2023, June 8). U.S. border asylum policy enters new territory post-Title 42. Migration Policy Institute. www.migrationpolicy.org (link)

Congressional Research Service. (2021, April 14). Deferred Action for Childhood Arrivals (DACA). www.congress.gov (link) Congress.gov

Congressional Research Service. (2023, September 21). The Biden Administration's final rule on arriving aliens seeking asylum (Parts 1 and 2). Congressional Research Service. crsreports.congress.gov (link)

Cornell Law School, Legal Information Institute. (n.d.). 22 U.S. Code § 2656 – Management of foreign affairs (Global Magnitsky Human Rights Accountability Act note).

www.law.cornell.edu (link)

Cortes Romero, L. (2020, April 27). Activism leads, the law follows: DACA and its fate at the Supreme Court. Human Rights Magazine, American Bar Association. www.americanbar.org (link)

Council on Foreign Relations. (2025, October 21). U.S. confrontation with Venezuela (Instability in Venezuela). Global Conflict Tracker.

www.cfr.org (link)

Department of Homeland Security v. Regents of the University of California, 591 U.S. ___ (2020). www.supremecourt.gov (link)

Department of Homeland Security. (2012, June 15). Exercising prosecutorial discretion with respect to individuals who came to the United States as children. www.dhs.gov (link)

Department of Homeland Security. (2023, May 11). Fact sheet: Circumvention of lawful pathways final rule. www.dhs.gov (link)

Donnelly, J. (2013). Universal human rights in theory and practice (3rd ed.). Cornell University Press. cornellpress.cornell.edu (link)

Donnelly, J. (2013). Universal human rights in theory and practice (3rd ed.). Cornell University Press.

cornellpress.cornell.edu (link) Cornell University Press

Electronic Privacy Information Center. (2023, March 28). EPIC comments: Circumvention of lawful pathways / CBP One NPRM. epic.org (link)

Elie Wiesel Genocide and Atrocities Prevention Act of 2018, Pub. L. No. 115-441, 132 Stat. 5586 (2019).

Congress.gov PDF (PLAW-115publ441.pdf)

European Parliament. (2022, June 9). European Parliament resolution of 9 June 2022 on the human rights situation in Xinjiang, including the Xinjiang police files (2022/2700(RSP)) [P9_TA(2022)0255].

www.europarl.europa.eu (link)

European Parliamentary Research Service. (2023). An EU ban on products made using forced labour (PE 739.356). European Parliament.

www.europarl.europa.eu (link))739356

European Union. (2024). Regulation (EU) 2024/3015 of the European Parliament and of the Council of 23 October 2024 on prohibiting products made with forced labour on the Union market. Official Journal of the European Union.

eur-lex.europa.eu (link)

Freeman, M. (2011). Human rights: An interdisciplinary approach (2nd ed.). Polity Press.

books.google.com (link)

Geneva Academy of International Humanitarian Law and Human Rights. (2016). Universality in the Human Rights Council: Challenges and achievements (Research brief).
www.geneva-academy.ch (link)

Georgetown Journal of International Affairs. (2025, May 14). Oil licenses and repression: The human rights impact of sanctions policy in Venezuela.

gjia.georgetown.edu (link)

Georgetown Public Policy Review. (2023, July 3). US sanctions are robbing Venezuelans of basic human rights.

gppreview.com (link)

Global Affairs Canada. (2021, January 12). Canada takes action regarding human rights violations in Xinjiang. Government of Canada.

www.canada.ca (link)

Global Centre for the Responsibility to Protect. (2025, November 14). Venezuela. Global Centre for the Responsibility to Protect.

www.globalr2p.org (link)

Global Magnitsky Human Rights Accountability Act, Pub. L. No. 114-328, div. A, title XII, subtitle F, 130 Stat. 2533 (2016) (codified at 22 U.S.C. Ch. 108).

uscode.house.gov (link)

Global Refuge. (2025, December 16). Global Refuge deeply alarmed by expansion of sweeping travel ban.
www.globalrefuge.org (link)

Greenberg, K. J. (Ed.). (2006). The torture debate in America. Cambridge University Press. www.cambridge.org (link)

Greitens, S. C., Lee, M., & Yazici, E. (2020). Counterterrorism and preventive repression: China's experience in Xinjiang. International Security, 44(3), 9–47.

scholar.google.com (link)

Heritage Foundation. (2025, March 31). The U.S. must re-design asylum law for 21st-century reality and put America first. The Heritage Foundation. www.heritage.org (link)

Human Rights First. (2025, January 10). Remain in Mexico: Unlawful, ineffective, and must never be repeated. Human Rights First. humanrightsfirst.org (link)

Human Rights Watch. (2004). The road to Abu Ghraib. Human Rights Watch. www.hrw.org (link)

Human Rights Watch. (2013, February 14). "The trouble with tradition": When values trample over rights. Human Rights Watch.

www.hrw.org (link)

Human Rights Watch. (2020). United States. In World report 2020. Human Rights Watch. www.hrw.org (link)

Human Rights Watch. (2021, April 27). A threshold crossed: Israeli authorities and the crimes of apartheid and persecution. Human Rights Watch.

www.hrw.org (link) Human Rights Watch

Human Rights Watch. (2021). "Break their lineage, break their roots": China's crimes against humanity targeting Uyghurs and other Turkic Muslims. Human Rights Watch.

www.hrw.org (link)

Human Rights Watch. (2022, February 4). US: Border program's huge toll on children. Human Rights Watch. www.hrw.org (link) White House. (2021, January 20). Proclamation on ending discriminatory bans on entry to the United States. bidenwhitehouse.archives.gov (link)

Human Rights Watch. (2024). World report 2024: Iran. Human Rights Watch.

www.hrw.org (link) Human Rights Watch

Human Rights Watch. (2025, April 30). Venezuela: Brutal crackdown since elections. Human Rights Watch.

www.hrw.org (link)

Human Rights Watch. (2025, February 1). Protected no more: China's harassment, surveillance, and intimidation of Uyghurs in Türkiye. Human Rights Watch.

www.hrw.org (link)

Human Rights Watch. (2025). World report 2025: Venezuela. In World report 2025. Human Rights Watch.

www.hrw.org (link)

International Commission on Intervention and State Sovereignty. (2001). The responsibility to protect. International Development Research Centre. responsibilitytoprotect.org (link)

International Court of Justice. (2012). Questions relating to the obligation to prosecute or extradite (Belgium v. Senegal), Judgment of 20 July 2012. www.icj-cij.org (link)

International Rescue Committee. (2024, November 1). What do President Biden's border policies mean for asylum seekers? International Rescue Committee. www.rescue.org (link)

Keck, M. E., & Sikkink, K. (1998). Activists beyond borders: Advocacy networks in international politics. Cornell University Press. cornellpress.cornell.edu (link)

Kron, J. (2013). The Atrocities Prevention Board: Recommendations for improving U.S. government responses to atrocities (Issue brief). Center for American Progress.

cdn.americanprogress.org (link)

Lim, P. J. (2025). Combatting Uyghur forced labor: Trade law, supply chains, and human rights. Utah Law Review, 2025(2), 305–352.

scholar.google.com (link)"Combatting+Uyghur+forced+labor\"

Lutheran Immigration and Refugee Service. (2017, January 25). Lutheran Immigration and Refugee Service condemns the Trump administration's actions against refugees and migrants. Refugee Council USA. rcusa.org (link)

Mahmood, S. (2005). Politics of piety: The Islamic revival and the feminist subject. Princeton University Press.

press.princeton.edu (link)

Mayer, A. E. (2013). Islam and human rights: Tradition and politics (5th ed.). Routledge.

doi.org (link)

McDonnell, T. M. (2025). Unsafe at any speed: "Safe Third Country Agreements"—Offshoring and eroding legal protections owed to refugees and asylum seekers. Fordham Urban Law Journal, 53(1), 17. ir.lawnet.fordham.edu (link)

Médecins Sans Frontières. (2023, January 13). Inhumane migration policies endanger lives at the US-Mexico border. Doctors Without Borders. www.doctorswithoutborders.org (link)

Meissner, D., & Gelatt, J. (2020, June 26). The U.S. Supreme Court's DACA ruling: What happened and what's at stake for Dreamers and U.S. society. Migration Policy Institute. www.migrationpolicy.org (link)

Meyer, J. W., Boli, J., Thomas, G. M., & Ramirez, F. O. (1997). World society and the nation-state. American Journal of Sociology, 103(1), 144–181. doi.org (link)

Migration Policy Institute. (2025, April 24). In first 100 days, Trump has dramatic immigration changes. Migration Policy Institute. www.migrationpolicy.org (link)

Migration Policy Institute. (2025, October 15). Opening doors, hardening borders: Inside Biden's strategy on mixed migration and lessons for Europe. Mixed Migration Centre / Migration Policy Institute. (Cites DHS, "Fact sheet: Circumvention of lawful pathways final rule.") mixedmigration.org (link)

Millward, J. A., & Peterson, D. (2020). China's system of oppression in Xinjiang: How it developed and how to curb it. The Brookings Institution.

www.brookings.edu (link)

Miroff, N. (2020, November 25). U.S. border officials close Texas warehouse where chain-link "cages" for migrants became a symbol of mistreatment. The Washington Post. www.washingtonpost.com (link)

Moyn, S. (2010). The last utopia: Human rights in history. Harvard University Press. www.hup.harvard.edu (link)

Mudde, C. (2019). The far right today. Polity Press. politybooks.com (link)

Murphy, L., Elimä, N., & Hallam, E. (2020). In broad daylight: Uyghur forced labour and global supply chains. Helena Kennedy Centre for International Justice, Sheffield Hallam University.

www.shu.ac.uk (link)

Murray Osorio PLLC. (2024, November 1). Understanding the Biden Administration's Circumvention of Lawful Pathways Rule (CLP). www.murrayosorio.com (link)

Musawah. (2009). Framework for action: For equality in the family. Musawah.

www.musawah.org (link)

Mutua, M. (2001). Savages, victims, and saviors: The metaphor of human rights. Harvard International Law Journal, 42(1), 201–245. harvardilj.org (link)

National Immigration Law Center. (2025, January 24). Know your rights: Expedited removal expansion. www.nilc.org (link)

National Immigration Project of the National Lawyers Guild. (2023, May 26). Biden's asylum ban: Practice advisory. nipnlg.org (link)

Norris, P., & Inglehart, R. (2019). Cultural backlash: Trump, Brexit, and authoritarian populism. Cambridge University Press. doi.org (link)

Office of the United Nations High Commissioner for Human Rights. (n.d.-a). What are human rights? www.ohchr.org (link)

Office of the United Nations High Commissioner for Human Rights. (n.d.-b). Special procedures of the Human Rights Council. www.ohchr.org (link)

Office of the United Nations High Commissioner for Human Rights. (n.d.-c). Universal Periodic Review. www.ohchr.org (link)

Office of the United Nations High Commissioner for Human Rights. (2022, September 20). Report of the Independent International Fact-Finding Mission on the Bolivarian Republic of Venezuela (A/HRC/51/43). OHCHR.

www.ohchr.org (link)

Office of the United Nations High Commissioner for Human Rights. (2023, September 20). Venezuela: UN fact-finding mission says attacks on civic and democratic space continue. OHCHR.

www.ohchr.org (link)

Office of the United Nations High Commissioner for Human Rights. (2022a). Assessment of human rights concerns in the Xinjiang Uyghur Autonomous Region, People's Republic of China. OHCHR.

www.ohchr.org (link)

Office of the United Nations High Commissioner for Human Rights. (2022b, June 8). China must address grave human rights concerns and enable credible investigations – Bachelet. OHCHR.

www.ohchr.org (link)

Office of the United Nations High Commissioner for Human Rights. (1948). Universal Declaration of Human Rights. United Nations.

www.ohchr.org (link) OHCHR

Office of the United Nations High Commissioner for Human Rights. (1966a). International Covenant on Civil and Political Rights. United Nations.

www.ohchr.org (link) OHCHR

Office of the United Nations High Commissioner for Human Rights. (1966b). International Covenant on Economic, Social and Cultural Rights. United Nations.

www.ohchr.org (link) OHCHR

Office of the United Nations High Commissioner for Human Rights. (2024). Situation of human rights in the Islamic Republic of Iran (A/HRC/55/62). United Nations Human Rights Council.

www.ohchr.org (link)

Organization of Islamic Cooperation Independent Permanent Human Rights Commission. (2020). OIC declaration on human rights. Organization of Islamic Cooperation.

www.oic-iphrc.org (link)

Organization of Islamic Cooperation. (1990). Cairo Declaration on Human Rights in Islam. Organization of Islamic Cooperation.

www.oic-oci.org (link)

Our Secure Future. (2018). What you should know about the WPS Act of 2017 (Policy brief). Our Secure Future.

oursecurefuture.org (link)

Politico. (2025, November 29). Trump orders the closure of Venezuelan airspace. Politico.

www.politico.com (link)

Qiang, X. (2021). The road to digital unfreedom: President Xi's surveillance state. Journal of Democracy, 30(1), 53–67.

scholar.google.com (link)"The+road+to+digital+unfreedom\"

Renteln, A. D. (1990). International human rights: Universalism versus relativism. Sage.

us.sagepub.com (link)

Reuters. (2019, September 24). Trump calls on nations to reject globalism, embrace nationalism. Reuters.
www.reuters.com (link)

Reuters. (2025, April 28). Trump's first 100 days: America First president is overturning world order. Reuters. (URL format will depend on final article slug; any copied
www.reuters.com (link)

Reuters. (2025, November 24). U.S. labels another Venezuelan group as terrorist, ramping up boat strikes. Reuters.

www.reuters.com (link)

Ries, L. (2021). Rising from the ashes: Principles and policies for a new American immigration system. The Heritage Foundation. www.heritage.org (link)

Roberts, S. R. (2020). The war on the Uyghurs: China's internal campaign against a Muslim minority. Princeton University Press.

press.princeton.edu (link)

Ryan, S. (2021). Atrocity crimes in Xinjiang: Moving beyond legal labels. Global Responsibility to Protect, 13(3), 215–244.

scholar.google.com (link)"Atrocity+crimes+in+Xinjiang\"

Sen, A. (1997). Human rights and Asian values. The New Republic, 217(2–3), 33–40. (Stable copy via JSTOR or institutional access; public discussion at www.carnegiecouncil.org (link))

Sikkink, K. (2011). The justice cascade: How human rights prosecutions are changing world politics. W. W. Norton. wwnorton.com (link)

Sirriyeh, A. (2020). 'Dreamers', (un)deserving immigrants and generational interdependence. Population, Space and Place, 26(8), e2370. doi.org (link)

Texas Standard. (2025, January 24). Trump stopped usage of the CBP One app at the border. Here's what that means. www.texasstandard.org (link)

Tobin, D. (2022). Genocidal processes and social death in Xinjiang. Ethnic and Racial Studies, 45(9), 1635–1657.

scholar.google.com (link)"Genocidal+processes+and+social+death+in+Xinjiang\"

Trump v. Hawaii, 585 U.S. ___ (2018). www.supremecourt.gov (link)

Türk, V. (2025, June 11). UN rights chief warns of $60 million funding shortfall. Reuters. www.reuters.com (link)

U.S. Citizenship and Immigration Services. (2025, January 24). Consideration of Deferred Action for Childhood Arrivals (DACA). www.uscis.gov (link)

U.S. Congress. (2014). Venezuela Defense of Human Rights and Civil Society Act of 2014, Pub. L. No. 113-278, 128 Stat. 3011.

www.congress.gov (link)

U.S. Congress. (2017). Women, Peace, and Security Act of 2017 (Public Law 115–68). Congress.gov PDF (PLAW-115publ68.pdf)

U.S. Congress. (2019). Elie Wiesel Genocide and Atrocities Prevention Act of 2018 (Public Law 115–441). Congress.gov PDF (PLAW-115publ441.pdf)

U.S. Customs and Border Protection. (2024). Uyghur Forced Labor Prevention Act (UFLPA). U.S. Department of Homeland Security.

www.cbp.gov (link)

U.S. Department of Homeland Security. (2021, October 29). Termination of the Migrant Protection Protocols. www.dhs.gov (link)

U.S. Department of Homeland Security. (2023, May 11). Fact sheet: Circumvention of lawful pathways final rule. U.S. Department of Homeland Security. www.dhs.gov (link)

U.S. Department of Justice, Office of the Inspector General. (2021, January 14). Review of the Department of Justice's planning and implementation of its zero tolerance policy and its coordination with the Departments of Homeland Security and Health and Human Services(Evaluation and Inspections Division Report 21-028). U.S. Department of Justice. oig.justice.gov (link) of Form

U.S. Department of State. (2023). 2023 country reports on human rights practices: China (includes Hong Kong, Macau, and Tibet).

www.state.gov (link)

U.S. Department of State. (2023). Uyghur Forced Labor Prevention Act strategy and enforcement.

www.state.gov (link)

U.S. Department of State. (2023). Venezuela 2023 human rights report. Bureau of Democracy, Human Rights, and Labor.

www.state.gov (link)

U.S. Department of State. (2023). Women, Peace, and Security.

2021-2025.state.gov (link)

U.S. Department of State. (2024). 2024 country reports on human rights practices: Venezuela. Bureau of Democracy, Human Rights, and Labor.

www.state.gov (link)

U.S. Department of State. (2024). Country reports on human rights practices for 2023. U.S. Department of State.
www.state.gov (link)

U.S. Department of the Treasury, Office of Foreign Assets Control. (n.d.). Global Magnitsky sanctions. U.S. Department of the Treasury.

ofac.treasury.gov (link)

U.S. Department of the Treasury, Office of Foreign Assets Control. (n.d.). Global Magnitsky sanctions. U.S. Department of the Treasury.

ofac.treasury.gov (link)

U.S. Government. (2016). The United States National Action Plan on Women, Peace, and Security (2016 update).

1325naps.peacewomen.org (link)

U.S. Government. (2023). U.S. Strategy and National Action Plan on Women, Peace, and Security. The White House.

bidenwhitehouse.archives.gov (link)

UK Foreign, Commonwealth & Development Office. (2021, March 22). UK sanctions perpetrators of crimes against Uyghur Muslims in Xinjiang. Government of the United Kingdom.

www.gov.uk (link)

United Nations General Assembly. (2006). Human Rights Council (A/RES/60/251). undocs.org (link)

United Nations High Commissioner for Refugees. (1977). Note on non-refoulement (EC/SCP/2). UNHCR. www.unhcr.org (link)

United Nations Security Council. (1993). Resolution 827 (International Criminal Tribunal for the Former Yugoslavia) (S/RES/827). digitallibrary.un.org (link)

United Nations Security Council. (1994). Resolution 955 (International Criminal Tribunal for Rwanda) (S/RES/955). digitallibrary.un.org (link)

United Nations Sustainable Development Group. (n.d.). Human rights-based approach to development cooperation. unsdg.un.org (link)

United Nations. (1948). Universal Declaration of Human Rights (UN General Assembly Resolution 217 A (III)). www.un.org (link)

United Nations. (1951). Convention relating to the status of refugees, 189 U.N.T.S. 137. www.unhcr.org (link)

United Nations. (1951). Convention relating to the status of refugees. www.ohchr.org (link)

United Nations. (1966a). International Covenant on Civil and Political Rights. www.ohchr.org (link)

United Nations. (1966b). International Covenant on Economic, Social and Cultural Rights. www.ohchr.org (link)

United States Holocaust Memorial Museum. (2012, July 23). White House delivers update on genocide and mass atrocity prevention effort. Simon-Skjodt Center for the Prevention of Genocide.

www.ushmm.org (link)

United States Institute of Peace. (2012, April 26). Obama announces formation of the Atrocities Prevention Board.

www.usip.org (link)

Uyghur Forced Labor Prevention Act, Pub. L. No. 117-78, 135 Stat. 1525 (2021).

Congress.gov PDF (PLAW-117publ78.pdf)

Uyghur Human Rights Policy Act of 2020, Pub. L. No. 116-145, 134 Stat. 648 (2020).

Congress.gov PDF (PLAW-116publ145.pdf)

Uyghur Human Rights Project, & Ous Society for Central Asian Affairs. (2021). No space left to run: China's transnational repression of Uyghurs. Uyghur Human Rights Project.

uhrp.org (link)

Washington Office on Latin America. (2020, October 29). New report documents how U.S. sanctions have directly aggravated Venezuela's economic crisis. WOLA.

www.wola.org (link)

Washington Office on Latin America. (2023, May 12). 10 things to know about the end of Title 42. WOLA.
www.wola.org (link)

White House. (2011). Fact sheet: A comprehensive strategy and new tools to prevent and respond to atrocities [Press release on Presidential Study Directive-10].
obamawhitehouse.archives.gov (link)

White House. (2012, April 23). Fact sheet: A comprehensive strategy and new tools to prevent and respond to atrocities.

www.presidency.ucsb.edu (link)

White House. (2022). United States strategy on women, peace, and security. www.whitehouse.gov (link)

Women, Peace, and Security Act of 2017, Pub. L. No. 115-68, 131 Stat. 1202 (2017).

Congress.gov PDF (PLAW-115publ68.pdf)

About the Author

William J. Manosh is a political scientist and author. This is his third nonfiction title, following So Many Humans, Too Few Rights (2018) and So Many Humans, Too Few Rights:

Power, Policy, and the Limits of Universal Rights (expanded version, 2026).

He earned a Bachelor of Arts in Political Science from Florida Atlantic University, graduating with a 3.5 GPA, and completed graduate-level coursework in political science with a 3.67 GPA. His academic background emphasizes U.S. foreign policy, international law, and post–Cold War human-rights institutions.

The State of Modern-Day Human Rights extends his human-rights scholarship, examining how U.S. statutes, institutions, and political incentives translate rights language into policy outcomes.

pod-product-compliance